HUSO 2018

The Fourth International Conference on Human and Social Analytics

June 24 - 28, 2018

Venice, Italy

HUSO 2018 Editors

Dennis J. Folds Lowell Scientific Enterprises, USA

Jan Ole Berndt, Trier University, Germany

Printed from e-media with permission by:

Curran Associates, Inc.
57 Morehouse Lane
Red Hook, NY 12571

CURRAN ASSOCIATES INC. proceedings.com

Some format issues inherent in the e-media version may also appear in this print version.

Printed by Curran Associates, Inc. (2018)

International Academy, Research, and Industry Association (IARIA)
412 Derby Way
Wilmington, DE 19810

Phone: (408) 893-6407
Fax: (408) 527-6351

petre@iaria.org

Additional copies of this publication are available from:

Curran Associates, Inc.
57 Morehouse Lane
Red Hook, NY 12571 USA
Phone: 845-758-0400
Fax: 845-758-2633
Email: curran@proceedings.com
Web: www.proceedings.com

Table of Contents

HUSO 2018

Forward

The Fourth International Conference on Human and Social Analytics (HUSO 2018), held between June 24, 2018 and June 28, 2018 in Venice, Italy, aimed at bridging the concepts and the communities dealing with emotion-driven systems, sentiment analysis, personalized analytics, social human analytics, and social computing.

The recent development of social networks, numerous ad hoc interest-based formed virtual communities, and citizen-driven institutional initiatives raise a series of new challenges in considering human behavior, both on personal and collective contexts.

There is a great possibility to capture particular and general public opinions, allowing individual or collective behavioral predictions. This also raises many challenges, on capturing, interpreting and representing such behavioral aspects. While scientific communities face now new paradigms, such as designing emotion-driven systems, dynamicity of social networks, and integrating personalized data with public knowledge bases, the business world looks for marketing and financial prediction.

The conference had the following tracks:

- Social computing
- Social human analytics
- Social Analytics and Community Resilience

We take here the opportunity to warmly thank all the members of the HUSO 2018 technical program committee, as well as all the reviewers. The creation of such a high quality conference program would not have been possible without their involvement. We also kindly thank all the authors who dedicated their time and effort to contribute to HUSO 2018. We truly believe that, thanks to all these efforts, the final conference program consisted of top quality contributions.

We also gratefully thank the members of the HUSO 2018 organizing committee for their help in handling the logistics and for their work that made this professional meeting a success.

We hope that HUSO 2018 was a successful international forum for the exchange of ideas and results between academia and industry and to promote further progress in the area of human and social analytics. We also hope that Venice, Italy provided a pleasant environment during the conference and everyone saved some time to enjoy the unique charm of the city.

HUSO 2018 Chairs

HUSO Steering Committee

Els Lefever, Ghent University, Belgium
Dennis J. Folds, Georgia Tech Research Institute, USA
Nitin Agarwal, University of Arkansas at Little Rock, USA
Chen Ding, Ryerson University, Canada
Liz Bacon, University of Greenwich, UK

HUSO Industry/Research Advisory Committee

HUSO 2018

Committee

HUSO Steering Committee

Els Lefever, Ghent University, Belgium
Dennis J. Folds, Georgia Tech Research Institute, USA
Nitin Agarwal, University of Arkansas at Little Rock, USA
Chen Ding, Ryerson University, Canada
Liz Bacon, University of Greenwich, UK
Jan Ole Berndt, University of Trier, Germany
Christian Bourret, University of Paris East - Marne la Vallée (UPEM), France
Meena Jha, CQUniversity Sydney, Australia
Xiaolong Jin, 靳小龙, Chinese Academy of Sciences, China

HUSO Industry/Research Advisory Committee

Baden Hughes, GWI, Australia
Yi Shan, SDE II, Electronic Arts, Seattle, USA
Fan Yang, eBay Inc., USA
Massimiliano Zanin, The Innaxis Foundation & Research Institute, Madrid, Spain
Zhiwen Fang, Microsoft, USA

HUSO 2018 Technical Program Committee

Paul Abbiati, Founding Fellow of ELI - The European Law Institute, Austria
Nitin Agarwal, University of Arkansas at Little Rock, USA
Rodrigo Agerri, University of the Basque Country (UPV/*EHU*), Spain
Harry Agius, Brunel University London, UK
Ahmad T. Al-Taani, Yarmouk University, Irbid, Jordan
Hafizi Muhamad Ali, Yanbu University College, Saudi Arabia
Alessio Antonini, Università degli Studi di Torino, Italy
Saïd Assar, Telecom Ecole de Management, France
Arnulfo P. Azcarraga, De La Salle University, Philippines
Liz Bacon, University of Greenwich, UK
Lakshika Balasuriya, Kno.e.sis Center | Wright State University, USA
Panagiotis D. Bamidis, Aristotle University of Thessaloniki, Greece
Balbir Barn, Middlesex University, London, UK
Stefano Berretti, University of Florence, Italy
Shreyansh Bhatt, Kno.e.sis | Wright State University, USA
Christian Bourret, University of Paris East - Marne la Vallée (UPEM), France
Stefan Bratosin, Université Paul Valéry Montpellier 3, France
Luca Cagliero, Politecnico di Torino, Italy
María Luisa Carrió Pastor, Universitat Politècnica de València, Spain

Mario Cataldi, University of Paris 8, France
Chin-Chen Chang, Feng Chia University, Taichung, Taiwan
Bo-Hao Chen, Yuan Ze University, Taiwan
Dickson Chiu, The University of Hong Kong, Hong Kong
Yung Ryn (Elisha) Choe, Sandia National Laboratories, Livermore, USA
Aresh Dadlani, Gwangju Institute of Science and Technology (GIST), South Korea
Orphée De Clercq, LT3 | Ghent University, Belgium
Ibrahim Delibalta, Intel Corporation, USA / Koc University, Istanbul, Turkey
Engin Deniz Eris, Dokuz Eylül University, Turkey
Luigi Di Caro, University of Turin, Italy
Chen Ding, Ryerson University, Canada
Thierry Edoh, Technische Universität München/Applied Software Engineering, Germany
Joyce El Haddad, Université Paris Dauphine, France
Samy El-Tawab, James Madison University, USA
Zhiwen Fang, Microsoft, USA
Silvia Florea, Lucian Blaga University of Sibiu, Romania
Dennis J. Folds, Lowell Scientific Enterprises (LSE), USA
Paolo Garza, Politecnico di Torino, Italy
Feng George Yu, Youngstown State University, USA
Denis Gracanin, Virginia Tech, USA
William Grosky, University of Michigan-Dearborn, USA
Diofantos G. Hadjimitsis, Cyprus University of Technology, Cyprus
Malka N. Halgamuge, University of Melbourne, Australia
Hossein Hamooni, Visa Research, USA
Ragib Hasan, University of Alabama at Birmingham, USA
Takafumi Hayashi, The University of Aizu, Japan
Manolo Dulva Hina, ECE Paris School of Engineering, France
Tzung-Pei Hong, National University of Kaohsiung, Taiwan
Baden Hughes, GWI, Australia
Emilio Insfran, Universitat Politecnica de Valencia, Spain
Roberto Interdonato, Université de La Rochelle, France
Jaroslaw Jankowski, Wrocław University of Technology, Poland
Meena Jha, CQUniversity Sydney, Australia
Minhao Jiang, The Hong Kong University of Science and Technology, Hong Kong
Xiaolong Jin, Institute of Computing Technology (ICT) | Chinese Academy of Sciences (CAS), China
Mirko Kämpf, Cloudera, Inc., USA
Selvi Kannan, College of Business | Victoria University, Australia
Hassan A. Karimi, University of Pittsburgh, USA
Muhammad Khalid, Northumbria University, Newcastle Upon Tyne, UK
Konstantin Kuzmin, Rensselaer Polytechnic Institute (RPI), USA
Georgios Lappas, Western Macedonia University of Applied Sciences, Greece
Els Lefever, Ghent University, Belgium
Ken Li, Hong Kong Institute of Vocational Education, Hong Kong
Rita Yi Man Li, Hong Kong Shue Yan University, Hong Kong
Francesco Longo, Università degli Studi di Messina, Italy
Eurico Lopes, Instituto Politécnico de Castelo Branco, Portugal
Yutao Ma, Wuhan University, China
Christos Makris, University of Patras, Greece

Mahshid Marbouti , University of Calgary, Canada
Elvis Mazzoni, University of Bologna, Italy
Fernanda Monteiro Eliott, Vanderbilt University, USA
Jason R.C. Nurse, University of Oxford, UK
Jan Ole Berndt, University of Trier, Germany
Riccardo Ortale, ICAR - CNR, Italy
Carlos Enrique Palau Salvador, Universidad Politecnica de Valencia, Spain
Marinella Petrocchi, Istituto di Informatica e Telematica - CNR, Pisa, Italy
Rahim Rahmani, University of Stockholm, Sweden
Haricharan Ramachandra, LinkedIn, USA
Sebastian Robert, Fraunhofer-Anwendungszentrum Industrial Automation (IOSB-INA), Germany
Carsten Röcker, Fraunhofer Application Center Industrial Automation (IOSB-INA), Germany
George E. Raptis, University of Patras, Greece
Muhammad Hassan Raza, Dalhousie University, Canada
Priya Saha, Florida Institute of Technology, USA
Roberto Saia, University of Cagliari, Italy
Claudio Schifanella, University of Turin, Italy
Kristen Schuster, King's College London, UK
Samir Shah, Drexel University, USA
Yi Shan, SDE II, Electronic Arts, Seattle, USA
Filippo Simini, University of Bristol, UK
Agata Marta Soccini, University of Torino, Italy
L. Venkata Subramaniam, IBM Research, New Delhi, India
Sude Tavassoli, Kaiserslautern University of Technology, Germany
Juan-Manuel Torres-Moreno, Université d'Avignon et des Pays de Vaucluse, France
Carlos M. Travieso-González, Universidad de Las Palmas de Gran Canaria, Spain
Thrasyvoulos Tsiatsos, Aristotle University of Thessaloniki, Greece
Mihaela Tudor, Paul Valéry University, France
Lorna Uden, Staffordshire University, UK
Luis Alfonso Ureña López, Universidad de Jaén, Spain
Massimo Villari, Universita' di Messina, Italy
Liqiang Wang, University of Central Florida, USA
Xuebin Wei, James Madison University, USA
Sanjaya Wijeratne, Kno.e.sis Center | Wright State University, USA
Cong-Cong Xing, Nicholls State University, USA
Anbang Xu, IBM Research - Almaden, USA
Fan Yang, eBay Inc., USA
Massimiliano Zanin, The Innaxis Foundation & Research Institute, Madrid, Spain
Katharina Anna Zweig, TU Kaiserslautern, Germany

Copyright Information

Acquisition and Analyses of Lessons Learned from Social Network R&D Using Machine Learning

Marco Javier Suárez Barón
Research Department
University Corporation UNITEC
Bogotá, Colombia
marcosuarez@unitec.edu.co

Abdelraouf Ishtaiwi
Faculty of Information Technology
Petra University
Amman, Jordan
aishtaiwi@uop.edu.jo

Johan David Diaz Mendivelso
Faculty of Computing
UPTC University
Sogamoso, Colombia
johan.diaz@uptc.edu.co

***Abstract*—This article presents the development of a computational framework used for the extraction and recovery of lessons learned that have been extracted from academic and research related social networks; the lexical analysis applied is focused to Spanish language. The algorithm executes the lexical analysis using Natural Language Programming (NLP) techniques. The final result of the process shows that the use of this type of lexical and semantic analysis is a key component in tasks of social analysis, text mining and semantic enrichment.**

Keywords-Lexicon analysis; Semantic annotations; Machine Learning; Lessons learned; Social networks.

I. INTRODUCTION

Social networks are currently considered as the main tool for sharing information and data. In this research, information and data will be taken from lessons learned contained in specialized social networks focused on research and such as Research gate [1], LinkedIn [6] and Blogs [1]. Nevertheless, most of the research experiences and knowledge are not registered or used, and information is not being properly exploited in those networks.

As a solution for that, the use of computational models like Machine Learning or Deep Learning enables the structuring and integration of specialized knowledge acquired from significant experiences, such as lessons learned [7]. The application of these models allows for greater flexibility in the acquisition process and facilitates the capture, recovery, transfer, and reuse of knowledge. Implementing these technological platforms will provide the entire organizational structure with a crucial tool for decision-making and strategic planning on R & D issues.

The paper is structured as follows: Section 2 describes the theoretical background, which involves Knowledge Management (KM) process and methods, models to manage knowledge on social systems and Learning technologies and organizational strategies to exchange knowledge; Section 3 details our proposed framework to combine and summarize research information and data to obtain final lessons learned; Section 4 presents results and discussion on the main components and phases of this computational model desing. Finally, in Section 5, we present our main conclusions and further works.

II. BACKGROUND

The generation of new knowledge is used for decision-making in non-simulated and simulated environments within the Learning process in the network. Planned R & D entities are thus created to optimize processes, reduce costs, increase innovation, and consider new projects. Specifically, these entities will be the context in which individuals and the organization will learn more [2].

Despite scientific advances on this subject, there are still gaps in the analysis of information from social networks of investigative type whose content specifically covers issues related to science, technology and innovation. The social networks studied in this article and the information registered in these networks correspond specifically to academic, business and scientific social networks, although, for this work we used information contained in Twitter social network for the extracting and integrating process.

The application of Machine Learning enables the structuring and integration of specialized knowledge acquired from significant experiences, such as lessons learned [3]. The application of these models allows for greater flexibility in the acquisition process; it facilitates the capture, recovery, transfer, and reuse of knowledge.

Social media has increased interest in our daily activities, and the user profile of each individual is considered a significant source of information [3]. Both Web sites and social networks are potential tools for the management, updating, and exchange of information and knowledge in fields that are interested in knowing the basic thoughts, ideas, relationships and activities of each individual in their environment, such as marketing.

On the basis of this concept, Knowledge Management (KM) theories center on mechanisms to help maintain knowledge within an organization. According to [4], as KM theory evolved, different models were proposed for innovation management in companies from multiple sectors in France and Germany, which have led us to focus our work primarily on the concept of Personal Knowledge Management (PKM), one of the most recent lines of work in this field [5].

III. METHODOLOGY

In the framework purposed, the process-centered approach focuses on individuals, as the most significant source of knowledge within an organization, and upholds the idea of resolving the cooperation problems amongst them through a process to achieve their social commitment to transfer and share knowledge. The basic methods used in this approach, such as Computer-Supported Cooperative Work, Workflow Administration, or processes training, among others, seek to foster communication and collaboration between individuals.

The framework used in this research project enabled the authors to standardize concepts, practices, and criteria to apply to the proposed metamodel and served as a reference for confronting and resolving new test cases of a similar nature.

This framework also includes the promotion of new forms of knowledge capture, based on sources of information, such as lessons learned, that circulate in social networks. The generation of new knowledge is used for decision-making in non-simulated and simulated environments within the Learning process in the network. Planned R & D entities are thus created to optimize processes, reduce costs, increase innovation, and consider new projects.

Specifically, these entities will be the context in which individuals and the organization will learn more. The framework objectives described above are summarized in the functional components presented in Figure 1.

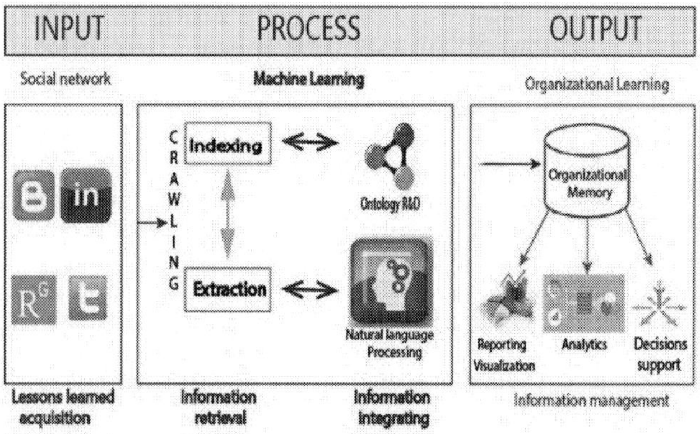

Figure 1. Learning and organizational knowledge framework

The acquisition and structure of a lesson learned, also known as *"pattern"* or relevant information in the metamodel, represents the relationship between the result of a process, project, indicators, conditions or causes that facilitated and / or hindered the strategic plan of R & D. In general, it is recommended to describe the finding in the past tense; however, the present can be used in those cases in which the effects and / or contexts continue to be valid. Figure 2 shows an example of lessons learned registered in social network Twitter.

Figure 2. Example of lessons learned registered in social network Twitter.

IV. RESULTS

To carry out the information extraction process, an application has been implemented for these three social networks; the application based, on Python-social-auth[6] technology, allows the development in an agile way and provides the connection to numerous social networks with little configuration of parameters; the social networks connected to framework are shown in Figure 1. The framework is integrated with certain profiles; this application allows access to tweets, retweets and mentions that refer to textual structures of topics related to R + D lessons. The text structures are identified with a # hashtag that will be defined by the research group or groups of researchers associated with the R + D centers.

The mathematical model applied to obtain the associated trends in each lesson learned identifies an entity named category. The entity defines relevant and not relevant topics in the R & D center; the mathematical model is shown in (1). The results can then be used to calculate aggregations, identify trends and produce reports, dashboards and performance measures.

$$A\chi = \sum_{n=1}^{\infty}(A, P, D) \qquad (1)$$

Where:

$A\chi$: Represents the content relevance for extracting. If the relation is equal to zero, then the lesson learned is not a candidate for acquisition.
P: Weight (I like it, comments): evaluates the number of likes or retweets linked to each lesson registered.
A: Relevant publications: Similarity R & D terms for *P*, e.g. Synonyms, folksonomies, Hashtags.
D: Registration time: Determines the timeline from lesson registered to first response; e.g. hours, days, minutes.
n: Number of arcs: Represents the thread or sequence for each lesson learned.

The knowledge management model continues with the implementation of a syntactical/morphological process of analysis, using the ontology-lexicon variation method, which has been combined with Natural Tool Kit Language (NTKL) [6], a natural language processing tool. When using NLTK, it was possible to separate each extracted lesson learned. In the syntactic/morphologic process of lessons learned, Spanish language grammar rules are applied, and we consider punctuation marks as key syntactic items, so that the reading of each one of the characters contained in texts related to lessons learned could be started/stopped; see equation (2). If each character (c) in a phrase is considered as a chain, and spaces separate each character are followed additionally, by a period and a space; then that phrase is considered as complying with the suggested structure.

$$P(c1\,c2\,c3..cn) = \prod_{i=2}^{n} P(ci|c1...ci-1) \qquad (2)$$

The tree grammar decomposition described in Figure 3 shows the semantic behavior for each word, each one regarded as an entity contained in the R & D data ontology; articles, connectors and linking words have been discarded in this analysis.

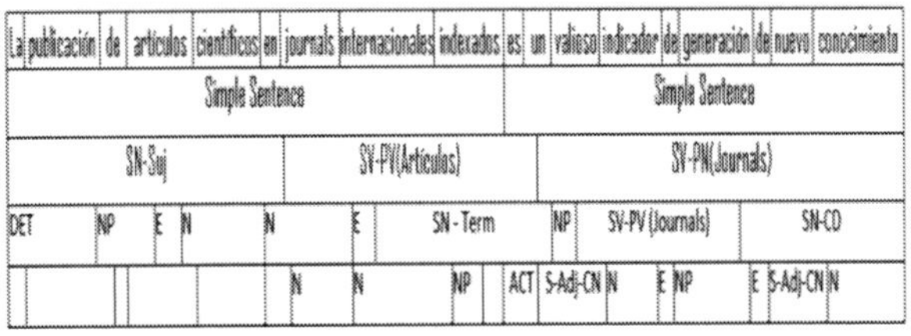

Figure 3. Lexical/morphological decomposition of a lesson learned

Figure 4 shows the standardized interface in order to optimize the ability to search, retrieve and analyze the texts of lessons learned extracted. In this case, the capture and extraction of texts from the Twitter social network is presented. The figure shows the user interface of the framework in its semantic analysis component. The result involves entities and concepts that are analyzed lexically and syntactically. Meanwhile, the semantic (structural) analysis given to each learned lesson made it possible to identify entities that are or are not contained within the R & D vocabulary.

Figure 4: Standardized interface in order to optimize the ability

Finally, Figure 5 shows the comparison of the trends of lessons learned regarding the strategic axes of the R & D centers. The analysis shows that in September there was a greater opinion tendency on R & D Management (45.76%) as in the month of October (33.93%) and the trend of publications with respect to R & D projects is greater, 75.00%.

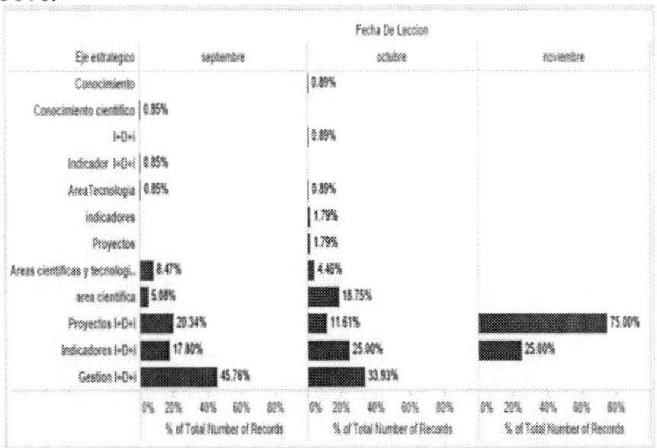

Figure 5: Comparison of the trends of lessons learned.

V. CONCLUSIONS AND FUTURE WORK

Lessons learned analysis from social network using Machine Learning allows for understanding the impact that perceptions and opinions shared by R & D social networks resources have in a series of experiences or pieces of knowledge, for instance, in technological surveillance. An R & D specialized social group can perform regular offline analysis, writing reports understanding the impact that perceptions and opinions shared by R & D social networks resources have in a series of experiences or pieces of knowledge, for instance, in technological surveillance, retrieved and formalized in real time. The research proposed in this paper makes it easier to incorporate the great volume of spontaneous and real time information provided by social networks, forums and blogs to assess its impact on trends and thematic behaviour, so that both critical events and competitive advantages could be discovered.

REFERENCES

[1] M. Suárez and B. Pico, "Framework of Organizational Learning in R&D centers, Supported by Lessons Learned", Advances in Information Sciences and Service Sciences, Vol.8, pp. 8-15, 2016, https://doi.org/10.4156/aiss.

[2] P. Różewski, J. Jankowski, P. Bródka, and R. Michalski, "Knowledge workers' collaborative Learning behavior modeling in an organizational social network" Computers In Human Behavior, pp. 1248-1260.

[3] T. Makkonen and T. Inkinen, "Innovation quality in knowledge cities: Empirical evidence of innovation award competitions in Finland", Expert Systems with Applications, Vol. 2 pp. 5597–5604, 2013.

[4] Sh. Liao and Ch. Wu, "System perspective of knowledge management, organizational Learning and organizational innovation", Expert Systems with Applications, Vol 4, pp. 1096–1103, 2013.

[5] R. Maruta, "The creation and management of organizational knowledge", Knowledge-Based Systems, Vol 3, pp. 26-34, 2014.

[6] M. Suárez and B. Pico, "Framework of Organizational Learning in R&D centers, Supported by Lessons Learned", International Journal of Applied Engineering Research, Vol.10, pp. 41744-41748, 2015

[7] P. Bermell-Garcia, W. Verhagen, S. Astwood and K. Krishnamurthy. "A framework for management of Knowledge-Based Engineering applications as software services: Enabling personalization and codification", Advanced Engineering Informatics, pp. 219-230, 2012.

Simulating Psychological Experiments: An Agent-Based Modeling Approach

Lukas Reuter, Jan Ole Berndt, Ingo J. Timm

Business Informatics 1
Trier University
54296 Trier, Germany
Email: [reuter,berndt,itimm]@uni-trier.de

***Abstract*—Analyzing human behavior in organizational structures becomes more difficult due to a rising complexity of teamwork processes and interdependencies between team members. The paper proposes an interdisciplinary approach of agent-based modeling and laboratory experiments from organizational psychology to overcome the shortcomings of each discipline and to allow a more detailed and realistic view on teamwork in theory and practice. To demonstrate the benefits of simulating psychological experiments, the replication of a small group experiment for analyzing the distribution of meta-knowledge is conducted. The results from simulation and experiment are plausible.**

Keywords*–*Agent-Based Modeling; Social Simulation; Team Mental Models; Meta-Knowledge.

I. Introduction

Due to rising complexity of teamwork processes, knowledge distribution and interrelationships between team members, understanding human behavior in organizational structures becomes more difficult. To overcome the shortcomings in analyzing teamwork, an interdisciplinary approach of Agent-Based Modeling (ABM) and theories from organizational psychology is promising to gain new insights. From a psychological perspective, theories and concepts of teamwork can be analyzed in laboratory experiments. The major drawbacks of these experiments are restrictions due to their limitations such as financial ones. ABM can be used to overcome the shortcomings and complement laboratory experiments, e.g., their design and scalability [1]. From an ABM perspective, modeling teamwork experiments can enable a more detailed comprehension of human behavior and should allow for more realistic agent architectures. One major characteristic of ABM is modeling behavior with specific actions which enables causal explanations of an observed pattern. However, in psychological research, experiments are commonly used to reveal correlations between conditions and measurements. Therefore, replicating a teamwork experiments with ABM supports psychologists to observe how behavioral team patterns emerge from individual actions [2].

The contribution of this paper is twofold: (1) how can ABM researcher and psychologists benefit from each other as well as what prerequisites are necessary to model and simulate psychological experiments and (2) presenting a study of replicating a teamwork experiment, which should clarify challenges and opportunities. The replicated study in this paper focuses on the different measurements (correlation vs. causality) in psychological research and ABM.

The remainder of this paper is structured as follows. In Section II, psychological research methods in a simulation context are shown. Section III presents an experimental study which utilizes a measurement: the Team Mental Model index (TMM Index) to analyze the distribution of meta-knowledge in teams and its consensus among team member. Consequently, an agent-based model of the TMM Index experiment is shown in Section IV. In Section V, a comparison of the results from experiment and simulation is given.

II. Simulating Psychological Experiments: Foundations and Challenges

Psychological research focuses on human cognition and behavior. In that context, experiments reveal correlations between controlled conditions and observable behavior (independent and dependent variables). Those correlations represent generalizable behavioral patterns, which can be utilized to indirectly draw conclusions about psychological constructs of human cognition for individuals and small groups.

Various scholars have proposed computer simulation in general and ABM in particular as a method in the field of psychology. However, these simulation studies can only provide insights into artificial systems as modeled and represented in a computer. Consequently, two questions arise. Firstly, why should psychological experiments be simulated since a computer does not exhibit human behavior? Secondly, how should these experiments be simulated, i.e., what are challenges and existing practices of modeling and simulating psychological experiments? The following two sections explore these questions and provide an overview of existing research in that area.

A. *Why Simulate Psychological Experiments?*

There are three main benefits of simulating psychological experiments. These roughly correspond to the following three phases of a computer simulation study.

1) The model development phase
2) The experiment and simulation design phase
3) The experimentation and results analysis phase

Activities in each of these simulation phases can both contribute to psychological research. Vice versa, simulating psychological experiments throughout these phases can also provide novel impulses for social simulation as a research method.

The first benefit of simulating experiments is their contribution to formal procedures and theory building. Due to the necessity to formalize the experiment in a computational model, such a simulation enforces a rigorous formulation of independent and dependent variables as well as the underlying theoretical constructs and their interrelations. The variables denote which conditions are manipulated during an experiment and which measurements are taken. These measurements are then used to conclude on underlying theoretical constructs which cannot be observed directly. However, in a simulation, these must be explicitly modeled in order to create observable effects. Consequently, developing simulation models requires explicating these constructs in a computable form. This supports precise descriptions of both psychological experiments and theory. In turn, precisely formalized psychological theory and cognitive or behavioral models can help building better social simulations. To be realistic, such simulations must be grounded in actual human cognition and behavior. Psychological experiments provide this grounding.

The second benefit covers the design of both experiments and simulations. In organizational as well as social psychology, experiments frequently involve groups of people and their interactions. To enable statistically relevant conclusions, each combination of independent variables must be sampled often enough. Every test must be repeated with at least 30 groups. Given a minimal group size of three persons, this kind of research requires at least 90 test persons per experiment condition; e.g., 360 persons for a simple 2x2 experiment design. Thus, it rapidly becomes unfeasible to scale up either the number of independent variables or the group size. Simulating experiments can help solve this problem since the number of agents in a model can be scaled up easily. If such a simulation is grounded in actual experiments, scaling it up may reveal interesting effects in the observed artificial system. These can then be used to design further experiments to verify or reject those findings. The experiments can then be reduced to the specific conditions that produce the respective effects in the simulation. Hence, the problem of scalability is alleviated. Moreover, the results provide additional validation of the simulation model or reveal the requirement for its refinement. This leads to a iterative experimentation process in which psychological experiments provide new hypotheses for the design of simulation studies and simulation results inspire additional laboratory experiments.

The third benefit of psychological experiment simulation is its contribution to the analysis of either method's results as well as to deriving and testing theoretical concepts. In psychology, experiments are used to reveal correlations between manipulated conditions and measurements to conclude on underlying theoretical concepts. However, these correlations cannot provide causal explanations of the observed effects. By contrast, computer simulations require the modeling of causality. Such a model provides a possible candidate for an explanation. While its correctness cannot be proven, it can be assumed to be feasible as long as it can replicate experiment results. Therefore, simulating experiments helps both developing and testing psychological theory as well as verifying measurements and results of social simulations.

Nonetheless, there are several challenges to be overcome for achieving the aforementioned benefits. The following section discusses existing research and identifies the challenges which will be addressed in the remainder of this paper.

B. Related Work

In order to simulate psychological experiments, it is necessary to transform these experiments into computational models and social simulation studies. Despite the recognition of ABM as a research method in (organizational and social) psychology, few researchers have attempted this so far. Instead, the majority of existing work focuses solely on simulation models of teamwork processes or on cognitive agent architectures. Thus, there is little work available on the challenge of transforming experiments into simulations and vice versa. Nevertheless, the following works in this context are noteworthy.

The majority of related work focuses on the development and exploration of conceptual models for explaining behavioral processes. This approach is primarily used for theory building by studying how the modeled interactions change within a simulation. It usually starts with a theoretical concept of cognition and behavior for the addressed application area which is then transferred into a computational model. For instance, Ren et al. model the meta-knowledge in teams to systematically explore when it is beneficial to know what other team members know in an agent-based simulation [3]. Similarly, Smith & Collins use such a simulation to analyze the impact of social contexts on distributed cognition processes [4]. Thus, both of these studies focus on model development to gain a more thorough understanding of theoretical concepts and their interplay.

Another line of research covers on the simulation design phase. Instead of being strictly theory-driven, those approaches focus on parameterizing individual agents from survey data. They use this data for creating unique profiles, which control the respective agents' decision-making in a social simulation [5]. While such an approach is more common for analyzing large populations [6], Kangur et al. make use of that technique to model influence factors and decision-behaviors for the acceptance of electric cars [7]. This contribution provides interesting insights into the transfer of variables in the form of survey items into parameters for artificial agents in a simulation setting.

The aforementioned approaches follow the recommended pattern of developing a model from theoretical concepts, implementing it, and parameterizing it using empirical data [2] [8]. However, none of them combines simulations with laboratory experiments. In that regard, Grand et al. complement those works by starting from a theory-driven model and then conducting an experiment to verify that model [9]. They first analyze processes of knowledge emergence in teams in a computer simulation and then compare the results with those gained from experiments with human subjects. Consequently, they contribute to the results analysis phase of experimentation and simulation.

While the discussed related work covers all of the benefits of simulating experiments, a direct replication of an experiment in a simulation has not yet been attempted. Especially the advantage of scaling up experiments and exploring different settings in a simulation for further experiment design remains unused. To achieve that, it is necessary to transform the settings of an existing experiment into simulation inputs and outputs similar to using survey data for agent parameterization. In addition, the available information and the decision-making of these agents must be specified. To that end, an appropriate abstraction of knowledge and interaction between these agents is required. Only then can the resulting model be used to replicate an experiment as well as varied to explore alternative settings. In the following, such a study is presented which shows how these challenges can be met.

III. Application: Team Mental Models for Expertise Location

In order to show the benefits and challenges of simulating psychological studies, an experiment is needed with: (1) a remote set of variables and (2) with relevance for ABM. Therefore, we choose an experiment which analyzes the distribution of meta-knowledge between team members. For team processes the knowledge of each team member is important to team performance [10]. Besides task related knowledge, the perspective of "who knows what in the team" (meta-knowledge) is also essential. In the past, studies showed positive effects of high meta-knowledge and team performance [11] [12]. Therefore Ellwart et. al. developed a valid and economic measurement for expertise location in organizational context, the TMM Index [13]. They conducted a study which validates the TMM Index in an experimental as well as a longitudinal field study. The TMM Index is a measure of team mental models based on the location of team member expertise. The measure integrates the quality of meta-knowledge and team consensus of within-team expertise. TMM is a subjective measure of individuals' perceived knowledge of team members' expertise (e.g., "I have a good 'map' of other team members' talents and skills"). Replicating the TMM Index experiment in an ABM has two benefits. On the one hand, with the use of ABM it is possible to analyze different experiment setups and examine if the same effects hold for e.g., larger group sizes. Therefore a plausible agent-based model is needed. On the other hand, teamwork plays an important role in ABM. In an ABM a team of agents can work together solve a particular task cooperatively. To that end, agents need a mutual beliefs of the skills and knowledge of other agents to coordinate successfully and efficiently [14]. Especially in recognizing the need to solve a task cooperatively, meta-knowledge can enhance the process. A measurement which indicates the quality of meta-knowledge is desirable for agent-based systems.

The original experimental study (N = 120, 40 teams) was conducted with university students. Participants worked in three-person teams to solve a decision-making task. The experimental task described the setting of working at a company that analyses weather data to evaluate travel routes and give recommendations to customers. Each participant received specific customer requests regarding three possible travel routes. The routes each consisted of three different stations. Each station was described by three weather properties (e.g. wind, temperature, and rain). Each participant was assigned expertise for one specific weather property, e.g. expertise for temperature, which included all information concerning the temperature at a given location. Expertise information was only visible to the assigned expert. Information concerning the other participants' expertise was presented as missing values. In order to create interdependence between team members and to process a customer request (e.g. customer 1: warm, dry, calm weather for swimming), all team members had to exchange information. Team members had to solve the tasks individually while cooperating concerning information exchange, which was crucial for processing a customer request. The experiment consisted of three phases. In the first phase each participant received individualized information about their expertise, weather properties, as well as the customer requests. In the second phase participants communicated via email to get the necessary information from other experts. In the third phase, each participant chose the best travel route for their customer request. In Figure 1, the travel routes which where used in the experiment are shown.

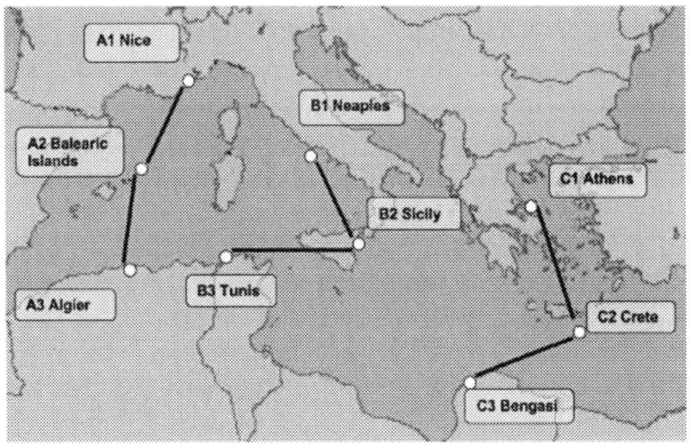

Figure 1. Travel Routes in Group Experiment

In order to validate the TMM Index, meta-knowledge and consensus about meta-knowledge was manipulated in a 2x2 design ("high" vs. "low" meta-knowledge). This resulted in (i) teams with high quality of meta-knowledge and high team consensus (all participants knew which team member received information and knew that all other team member received this information); (ii) teams with low meta-knowledge and high consensus (no participants received information about the expertise location but all participants knew that no one else received this information); (iii) teams with high meta-knowledge and low consensus (two participants received information about the expertise of other team members but no one was given information about what other team members were/were not told); and (iv) teams with low meta knowledge and high consensus (only one of the three team members received expertise information but all were informed that only one member received said information and were told which member).

The TMM index used in the laboratory experiment is based on a 7-point Likert-scale and is calculated using four items ("I have a good 'map' of other team members' talents and skills," "I know which team members have expertise in specific areas," "I know what task- related skills and knowledge each team member possesses," and "I know who on the team has specialized skills and knowledge that are relevant to me"). The calculation of the TMM Index is defined as follows:

$$TMM\ Index = \frac{\sum_{i=1}^{n} x_i}{n} - \sqrt{\frac{\sum_{i=1}^{n} (x_i - \mu)^2}{n}} \quad (1)$$

The index results in the subtraction of the mean value of the survey and the standard deviation and therefore also defined on a 7-point scale. The main hypothesis for the studies is to show if the TMM Index differentiates between teams with high knowledge and high consensus versus high knowledge and low consensus as well as between teams with low knowledge and low consensus and low knowledge and high consensus. The results of the experiment show that the hypothesis can be verified and the index is sensitive to meta-knowledge and consensus (for more detailed results see Section V).

IV. Agent-Based Model for Simulating Meta-Knowledge Distribution

In theory, subjective measurements from participants in a laboratory experiments are based on theirs observations from underlying processes or their knowledge combined with emotions. The original study implemented the TMM as a subjective measure, however in ABM, the TMM Index has to be based on objective knowledge or behavior (e.g., how agents communicate between each other). For reasons of simplification our first simulation only focused on the effects of high vs. low meta-knowledge on TMM Index. Thus, the goal of the ABM was to investigate whether the (objective) TMM Index in the simulation shows a similar sensitivity to manipulated changes of meta-knowledge as the perception based measure in the original experiment. The agent-based model is structured according to the setup of the laboratory experiment. In Figure 2, the components of the ABM are shown. On the left hand side, the input parameters for model configuration are shown. These parameters are based on the laboratory experiment and its scalability potential. On the right hand side, the output parameters, which are used to measure the TMM Index, are shown. In the center, the agent behavior is depicted which is modeled like the participants' behavior from the experiment. The agent's decision-making process is described in the next paragraphs detailedly.

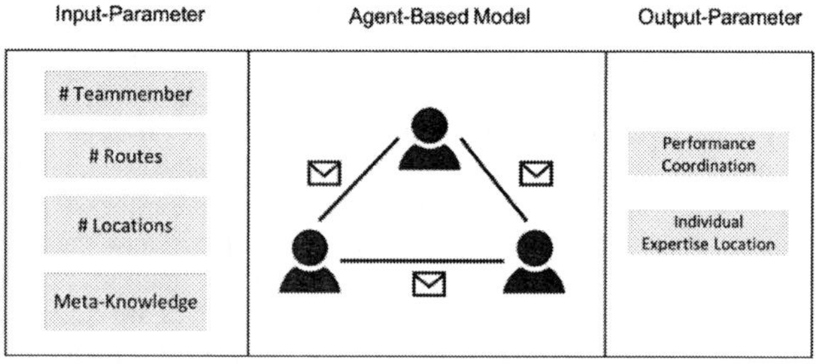

Figure 2. Agent-Based Model for Expertise Location

One major disadvantage of laboratory experiments is their limited scalability due to e.g. personnel or financial limitations. Therefore, the input parameters of the model are the number of team members, number of routes, number of locations, as well as actual meta-knowledge to analyze the results for larger team configurations. The output of the simulation is the TMM Index. The agent-based model itself consists of reactive agents with a representation of meta-knowledge. The knowledge about the expertise location for an agent is defined as follows for $\forall w \in Weatherproperty$:

$$Expertise(w) \rightarrow \begin{cases} Agent\ a; & a\ is\ an\ Expert\ for\ w \\ \emptyset; & guessing\ an\ Expert \end{cases} \tag{2}$$

For every team member each agent knows if they are experts for a particular kind of weather data. This representation determines if an agent has high or low meta-knowledge. In a case of high meta-knowledge, individual agents know exactly which team member holds what kind of weather information. In case of low meta-knowledge, an agent has no information concerning the expertise of other team members. Besides meta-knowledge, each agent has knowledge about weather conditions for different locations on travel routes. The following example in 3 shows the knowledge for a travel route consisting of three different location and each location is describes by three different weather properties.

$$\text{Location} \times \text{Weatherdata} = \begin{bmatrix} -1 & 5 & -1 \\ -1 & 2 & -1 \\ -1 & 6 & -1 \end{bmatrix} \tag{3}$$

The example shows the knowledge of an expert for the second weather property, e.g., rain. The evaluation of a weather property for locations is represented by a value from 1 to 9 which describes the suitability of this location for a specific customer request. A higher value shows a higher similarity. A value of -1 denotes missing information. The overall evaluation value for a route is the sum of the single ratings of the weather properties. L denotes the set of Locations and W denotes the set of weather properties:

$$RouteValue(R) = \sum_{i=1}^{L}\sum_{j=1}^{W} r_{ij} \tag{4}$$

The route with the highest overall rating is proposed to the customer. In order to calculate the route ratings for a customer request each agent can perform different actions which are modeled in the process from Figure 3:

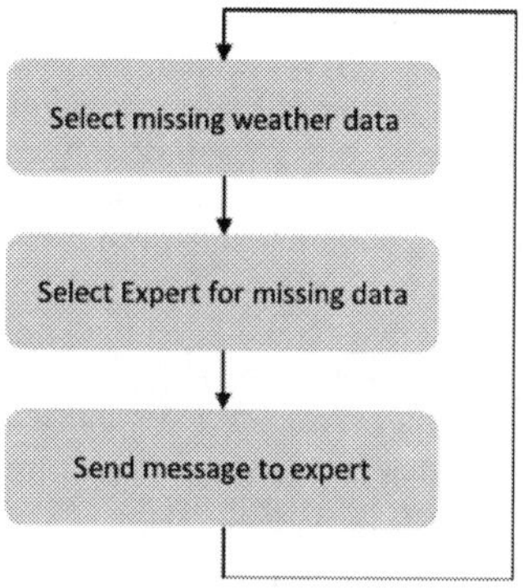

Figure 3. Process of Requesting Expert Information

The process is iterative and ends if an agent has no missing weather data left or has requested this information. In the second step the meta-knowledge determines which expert is requested. If an agent has no information about the expertise location, i.e., has low meta-knowledge it messages every team member. In Figure 4 the processing of messaging is shown. As communication protocol between agents FIPA ACL is used. In order to manage the information exchange agents use FIPA performatives. In this scenario "request", "inform" and "refuse" are applied. Each agent is able to get requests on missing information as well as informs on requested information. In case of a refuse, which means the requested information cannot be provided no action is performed. If there is no missing information left in the knowledge base, then each agent calculates the best route for the customer request.

The main issue of measuring the Index is to transform the subjective measure (4 item survey) into an objective

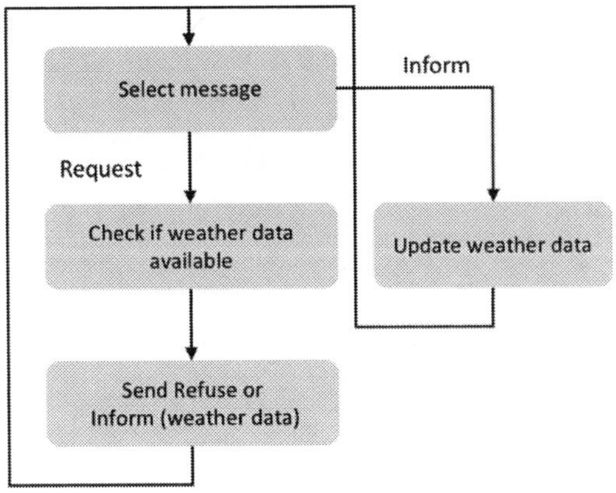

Figure 4. Processing Messages in Agents

measurement. To that end, the individual expertise of an agent is compared to the actual knowledge distribution to cover the 4 item measurement. Besides that, in the laboratory experiment, the highest correlation of TMM Index was measured with the coordination performance. Therefore, the TMM Index calculation in the simulation is based on the average of individual versus actual expertise location distribution (equation 5).

$$Expertise_a(w) \rightarrow \begin{cases} 1; & if\ indivual\ and\ actual \\ & Expertise\ are\ equal \\ 0 & no\ match \end{cases} \quad (5)$$

The actual TMM Index in the simulation is calculated as the difference of the mean average of the expertise matches and their standard deviation multiplied by the coordination performance. The coordination performance is represented as the ratio of positive requests and total amount of messages. It is used as an indicator for the performance of the underlying teamwork process. In order to test the model's plausibility to represent the TMM Index, the next Section show results from simulating the original experiment.

V. Results and Discussion

The simulation model is implemented in Java using the Repast Simphony Framework. To test for comparability and plausibility of the two methods, we compared simulation based TMM Index scores in the two conditions (high vs. low meta-knowledge) with TMM Index scores from the original study. The results are described in Section V-A. Additionally, the examination of the models behavior regarding the group size is shown in Section V-B.

A. Psychological Experiment versus ABM Simulation

In order to compare the results from the original experiment and the ABM, the simulation uses the same configuration (3 routes, 3 agents, 3 locations per route as well as high / low meta-knowledge). In case of a high meta-knowledge, each agent knows exactly which other agents are experts for. In case of low meta-knowledge there is no information about the expertise location provided. To measure the equivalence of simulation and experiment, the simulation output was transformed to a 7-point rating. The simulation was executed 1000 times. Simulation results are displayed in Table I.

TABLE I. TMM INDEX RESULTS ORIGINAL EXPERIMENT AND ABM SIMULATION

	Experimental Manipulation	
	Low Meta-Knowledge	High Meta-Knowledge
Subjective TMM Index in original experiment	3,05	4,36
TMM Index in ABM Simulation	2,64	7,00

Similar to the laboratory experiment, the TMM Index calculated in the simulation can distinguish between high and low meta-knowledge, with a lower TMM Index in the low meta-knowledge condition and a high Index in the high meta-knowledge condition (low meta knowledge: experiment 3.05, simulation 2.64; high meta-knowledge: experiment 4.36, simulation 7.00). In the high meta-knowledge condition, the simulation results overestimated the TMM Index. This is due to the direct measure of TMM used in the simulation. In contrast, the experimental study used a subjective measure of participants' perceived TMM. Unsurprisingly, with complete agreement of knowledge of expertise location in the ABM simulation, high meta-knowledge teams reached the maximum score of 7.00 on the TMM Index with zero standard deviation. An overview of the results is shown in Figure 5. In the low

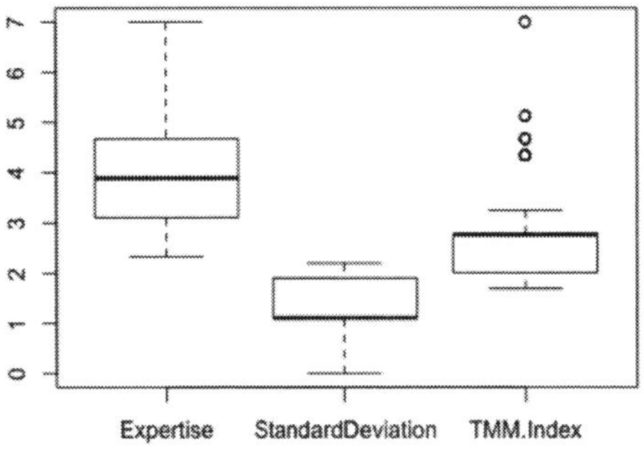

Figure 5. TMM Index Results of Simulation with Low Meta-Knowledge

meta-knowledge condition, the simulation based TMM Index was lower compared to the experimental results. Thus, we presume the different methods of measurement and abstraction caused the described differences in TMM Index. Moreover, the experiment measured a larger set of variables as the simulation model. Concerning the deviation of the meta-knowledge distribution, the computed results show similar characteristics (mean deviation simulation 1,23 and Experiment 1,36). Consequently, choosing an expert at random fits the observations of the empirical study for low meta-knowledge. Nevertheless, the

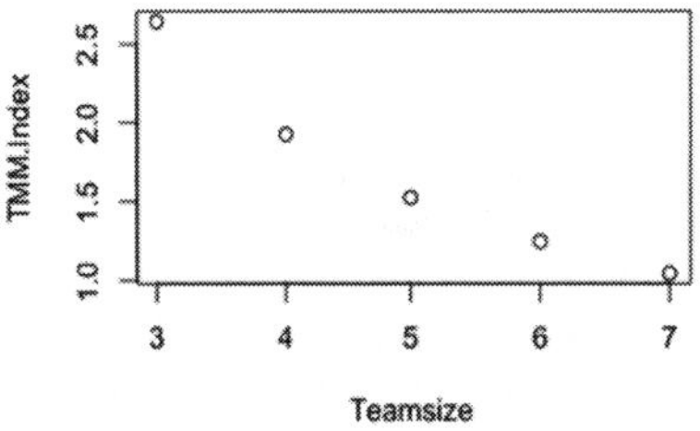

Figure 6. TMM Index results with increased Number of Group Members

results show that it is possible to transfer the concept of meta-knowledge measurement to agent-based systems. The simulation results for low meta-knowledge showed high consistency with the experiment and are plausible according to the concept of TMM Index.

B. Increasing sample size with ABM

In further simulations, we investigated how the TMM Index would change for low meta-knowledge teams with a varying number of team members (team size of 3 to 7 individuals; results are shown in Figure 6). Results show that with an increasing number of team members, the TMM Index decreases. In smaller teams, agents are more likely to select the correct expert at random as the number of possible experts is also smaller. Additionally, the ratio of coordination performance is decreasing due to an increased number of team members.

In total, the result for scaled experiments are plausible in the way that missing meta-knowledge has more negative effects on a team's performance than in smaller groups. The scaled experiment results show that the effect of an objective measurement of the TMM Index can distinct meta-knowledge distribution among team members more clearly. Consequently, measuring an objective TMM Index in the next laboratory experiment could produce more accurate results.

VI. Conclusion and Future Work

Using agent-based modeling to complement psychological research is a promising approach with up- and downsides. This paper presents an ABM which models a psychological experiment on meta-knowledge distribution in small groups. The experiment is used to validate the TMM Index, which is a subjective measurement to distinguish a team's meta-knowledge as well as its consensus about this meta-knowledge. In order to calculate the TMM Index for an agent-based simulation model it is objectified so that causal relationships between a team's performance and meta-knowledge could be shown. The TMM Index calculated from the simulation output is able to differentiate high and low meta-knowledge. Additionally, the simulation experiments revealed that the TMM Index can distinguish between high and low meta-knowledge in teams with larger group sizes, too. Due to the model's assumptions and restrictions, the TMM Index simulation results are plausible but overestimate the index. The major challenge in replicating this experiment is the transformation of the subjective TMM Index measurement to an objective one which represents a shift in not only measuring correlations but causality of teamwork processes and meta-knowledge. The presented study in this paper is a first step towards the vision of simulating psychological experiments realistically.

Future studies should aim to test if a more complex agent architecture is able to reproduce the results more accurately by integrating a consensus component in agents with different manifestations of meta-knowledge in form of different or mutual beliefs is promising. Moreover, ABM can not only be used to support design, formalization and analysis of experiments but complement conducting experiments. In a hybrid experiments with a valid agent-based model humans can interact with agents [15]. Such an approach could overcome limitations of laboratory experiments especially in formalizing measurements as well as modeling causality.

Acknowledgments

The project *AdaptPRO: Adaptive Process and Role design in Organisations* (TI 548/-1) is funded by the German Research Foundation (DFG) within the Priority Program "Intentional Forgetting in Organisations" (SPP 1921).

References

[1] I. J. Timm et al., "Towards multiagent-based simulation of knowledge management in teams." in Flexible knowledge practices and the Digital Workplace (FKPDW). Workshop within the 9th Conference on Professional Knowledge Management, M. Leyer, A. Richter, and S. Vodanovich, Eds. KIT: Karlsruhe, 2017, pp. 25–40.

[2] E. R. Smith and F. R. Conrey, "Agent-based modeling: A new approach for theory building in social psychology," Personality and social psychology review, vol. 11, no. 1, 2007, pp. 87–104.

[3] Y. Ren, K. M. Carley, and L. Argote, "The contingent effects of transactive memory: When is it more beneficial to know what others know?" Management Science, vol. 52, no. 5, 2006, pp. 671–682.

[4] E. R. Smith and E. C. Collins, "Contextualizing person perception: Distributed social cognition." Psychological Review, vol. 116, no. 2, 2009, p. 343.

[5] T. Balke and N. Gilbert, "How do agents make decisions? a survey," Journal of Artificial Societies and Social Simulation, vol. 17, no. 4, 2014, p. 13.

[6] N. E. Williams, M. L. OBrien, and X. Yao, "Using survey data for agent-based modeling: design and challenges in a model of armed conflict and population change," in Agent-Based Modelling in Population Studies. Springer, 2017, pp. 159–184.

[7] A. Kangur, W. Jager, R. Verbrugge, and M. Bockarjova, "An agent-based model for diffusion of electric vehicles," Journal of Environmental Psychology, vol. 52, 2017, pp. 166–182.

[8] J. C. Jackson, D. Rand, K. Lewis, M. I. Norton, and K. Gray, "Agent-based modeling: A guide for social psychologists," Social Psychological and Personality Science, vol. 8, no. 4, 2017, pp. 387–395.

[9] J. A. Grand, M. T. Braun, G. Kuljanin, S. W. Kozlowski, and G. T. Chao, "The dynamics of team cognition: A process-oriented theory of knowledge emergence in teams." Journal of Applied Psychology, vol. 101, no. 10, 2016, p. 1353.

[10] S. W. Kozlowski and G. T. Chao, "The dynamics of emergence: Cognition and cohesion in work teams," Managerial and Decision Economics, vol. 33, no. 5-6, 2012, pp. 335–354.

[11] J. R. Austin, "Transactive memory in organizational groups: the effects of content, consensus, specialization, and accuracy on group performance." Journal of applied psychology, vol. 88, no. 5, 2003, p. 866.

[12] A. B. Hollingshead, "Distributed knowledge and transactive processes in decision-making groups." in Composition., ser. Research on managing groups and teams, Vol. 1. US: Elsevier Science/JAI Press, 1998, pp. 103–123.

[13] T. Ellwart, U. Konradt, and O. Rack, "Team mental models of expertise location: Validation of a field survey measure," Small Group Research, vol. 45, no. 2, 2014, pp. 119–153.

[14] M. J. Wooldridge, Reasoning about rational agents. MIT press, 2000.

[15] L. Reuter, J. O. Berndt, and I. J. Timm, "Challenges of simulating teamwork in organizational scenarios," in 2017 Winter Simulation Conference (WSC), Dec 2017, pp. 4542–4543.

Identities, Motivations, Social Representations in Information and Communication Situations and Digital Society

The case of Santiago de Compostela Trippers

Christian Bourret and Joumana Boustany
DICEN IDF
University Paris East (UPEM)
Marne-la-Vallée - France
e-mails: {christian.bourret, joumana.boustany}@u-pem.fr

Abstract— **Compostela Ways constitute a highly publicised phenomenon of our ultra-modern society corresponding to a long tradition. In an information and communication approach insisting on meaning and interactions, we propose to analyse identities, motivations and social representations of the trippers. We focus on the digital aspects of the Compostela Ways, especially identity, traces and interactions on social networks as a new approach of this social phenomenon, analyzing their importance for the trippers as a specific manner to interact and give meaning to their trip in our individualist and consumerist society.**

Keywords - identities; social representations; digital society; social media; Santiago de Compostela.

I. Introduction

The Santiago de Compostela Pilgrim Way is a highly publicised phenomenon and it is part of a long tradition that goes back to the XIIth century [1]. After a long period of lethargy, for more than three centuries (1650 – 1980), the interest increased for the past forty years. In 1982, John Paul II was the first Pope to go to Santiago de Compostela. Since this visit, the number of people who obtained the "compostela" increased significantly: from 2491 trippers or hikers in 1985 to 7274 in 1991, 277,854 in 2016 and 301,036 in 2017 from 146 countries. The Compostela is an official certificate given by Santiago's archbishopric for pilgrims who did at least the last 100 km on foot or horseback, or the last 200 km by bicycle. For this purpose, pilgrims have to collect the stamps on the "Credencial del Peregrino" from the places they pass through to certify that they have been there. We use the words trippers or hikers, rather than pilgrims, which has a religious connotation. These hikers come from Spain (44.01%) Italy (16.06%), Germany (13.78%), USA (10.40%), Portugal (7.68%), France (5.24%), etc. [2]. As shown in the last available statistics, Santiago de Compostela is currently trendy all over the world. In addition to the growth rate of visitors and trippers, this interest is also shown by the number of publications: books, films, newspapers, etc. in various countries and languages.

With the ascent of social media, the community of Santiago de Compostela trippers adopted this mediation tools: Facebook, Twitter, Instagram, etc. as it was the case previously with websites.

In this paper, which is the first step in a larger project, we will focus on the digital identity of trippers and the issue of the "trace man", a concept defined by B. Galinon-Mélenec: "the 'trace man' would identify the Human of the 21st century, leaving everywhere traces of his passage and activities, likely tracked by merchants, watched to the detail by observers of all kinds, punished for any deviation to the norm... risking to raise legitimate concerns about the respect of privacy, the respect of individual freedoms and of the ethics" [3]. The virtual community of Compostela hikers, by communicating on Facebook, keep traces related to their experience, but also about their life. These traces allow creating the digital identity of the members of this community. Since the invention of the Internet, this issue has been subject to many publications. For Stutzman "the social network community fosters a more subjective and holistic disclosure of identity information" [4] even though it has been demonstrated that "In cyberspace the economies of interaction, communication, and coordination are different than when people meet face-to-face" [5].

In this paper, we study the presence of this community on Facebook. We address this issue in a multidisciplinary approach with a focus on the social representation theory. In fact "social representations provide criteria for evaluating the social environment that enable determination, justification or legitimization of certain behaviors" [6]. Social representations specifie a number of communicative mechanisms explaining how ideas are communicated and transformed into what is perceived as common sense and allows the understanding and interpretation of the digital identity of the Facebook Compostela Pilgrim.

II. Methodology

In this paper, we focused our study only on francophone Facebook pages considered as a public space. We excluded personal accounts as they belong to the private space as well as Facebook Groups that belong to both private and public spaces with closed and public groups. Our choice is also motivated by the characteristic of a Facebook page. It lets the page owner engage with people on Facebook as anyone can follow a page to get the public updates, even those who are not friends on Facebook.

To find relevant pages, we used the keyword "Compostelle". We have identified 78 Facebook pages related to our topic, the oldest one dating back to 2008 and being still active.

To be able to evaluate the activity of the selected pages, we used the online tool Likealyzer developed by Meltwater that measure 5 criteria:

- *Frontpage* which gives the first impression concerning the Facebook page.
- *About page*, which should contain milestones that give context of the page and contact information.
- *Activity* which gives the information type (text, photos, or videos), the number of posts per day, events, etc.
- *Response* which measures the interaction with visitors.
- *Engagement* which related to people talking or liking the page.

We will consider the "Compostela phenomenon" in a double perspective: search of meanings and analysis of the interactions between actors: "trippers", inhabitants and the role of information and communication technologies and social networks in the new sociability of the Compostela Ways. We also have a position of "engaged" or committed researchers [7] because one of the authors accomplished the Santiago de Compostela walk in 2011 and continues his observations and discussions with other walkers, interviews with Tourism Office members, with people in charge of Compostela Walkers' Associations, by specific documentary resources and by Websites and social media networks.

III. A PUBLICISED PHENOMENON ILLUSTRATING THE CONTRADICTIONS OF OUR SOCIETY

A. A privileged field to capture social representations and identity

Compostela Ways constitute a privileged field to clarify two key concepts in human sciences: social representations and identities. As defined by D. Jodelet [8], "social representations constitute an 'ordinary knowledge'. They describe, explain and recommend. They provide a method to interpret the reality, controlling our environment and driving us in society". For J.-C. Ruano-Borbalan [9], "we interpret the world continuously in the form of representations that the brain accumulates… they constitute reference mind systems to understand the world around us. The social representations constitute a key concept for Human Sciences that allow the interpretation of the mechanism of intelligence, the ideologies and mentalities."

B. The modern individualism crisis: a multiple and burst identity and questioning the sense of existence

Modernity, which has gradually been affirmed since the beginning of the sixteenth century in the West, has largely corresponded to the development of individualism to the detriment of collective institutions and traditions.

Having become an actor of his life in a secularized society, man has become responsible for his successes, as well as his failures [10]. In a "communicating society, but where people meet less and less" [11] the individual of social networks corresponds to a "connected individualism" [12], but where the ultra-connection does not prevent loneliness. It is in this context of a crisis of meaning, of "tiredness of being oneself" and of "connected individualism", that has developed, progressively since the 1980s, the "Compostela phenomenon", with a lot of ambivalence. This ambivalence corresponds to those of contemporary individualism that we are studying in our work.

IV. DIFFERENT MOTIVATIONS AND SOCIAL REPRESENTATIONS FOR DIFFERENT TYPOLOGIES OF TRIPPERS

According to Santiago's Archbishopric (2017), the motivations of the hikers obtaining the "Compostela" were religious 130,831 (43.46%), religious and cultural 142,662 (47.39%), only cultural 27,543 (9.15%). The majority of hikers are mainly "cultural hikers" more than pilgrims in the strict sense of the term, that is to say, with mixed religious and cultural motivations and, often the challenge of a personal experience to better understand oneself in interaction with others.

The motivations may be extremely diverse. It is often a willingness to review a turning point in life: divorce, bereavement, retirement or entering the active life for younger adults, especially Spanish. There are also various dimensions of a group trip or an individual trip: to be able to meet others and oneself, walking on a known and valued road linked with past, traditions and cultural heritage.

More generally, motivation is above all a search for meaning, in the ambient materialism of the consumer society. In addition, the motivation is a search for authenticity. We can cite the overworked executive director who forsakes his role, his social and hierarchical positioning for a period. Some may do the Way in response to a wish or for a sick person (intention).

There may also be cultural motivations: the Compostela Ways are a magnificent book of art history: Romanesque, Renaissance (Spanish "Plateresque") or Baroque, discovery of diverse landscapes, contact with nature, etc. Alternatively, there are also historical and traditional motivations: to walk the routes of thousands of pilgrims who have travelled these paths for more than a millennium.

Up to a certain point, Compostela Ways put the hikers, regardless of their social standing, on an equal footing, dealing with the challenges of a long-distance walk. However, some clues can be significantly revealing. There are those who sleep in the overcrowded refuges, those who prefer private inns and monasteries (more expensive but more comfortable), the various categories of hotels, those who carry all their necessities in their bags, those who have support cars ("coches de apoyo" in Spanish) from family's support or have received the services of transport companies step by step, etc.

The values of shared meaning and the quality of the relationships that fostered the rise of Christianity twenty centuries ago are reflected in the success of the Compostela Ways. They create shared meaning and a certain solidarity, often underlined, of people who do not know other people help each other and learn to walk together towards the same goal and sometimes stay together (couples form on the Ways).

The quality of relationships depends on the search for a certain authenticity. The language barrier is often easily overcome, as English has become the common language for the majority of trippers. For P. Nadal [13], "The Way... is not a simple walking way... (it is) an initiatory journey to the interior of oneself that would change the perception of many things... the disconnection with the superfluous, the communion of the body with nature... The pilgrimage can then be assimilated to a "semiotic machine" for the construction of a meaning to its existence.

V. Some Tracks for Interactions and Digital Identity on Social Networks

The Compostela Ways may both favor a collective approach or a search of loneliness but also often connected to a certain extent and especially with the development of mobile Internet. Like brotherhoods and chapels in the past, then websites, social media allows hikers to give advice, provide addresses, express feelings and emotions, and to surround themselves with their impressions and pictures. We found 78 francophone pages on Facebook, the first one dating back to 2008. Since then, the number of pages has grown every year (See Figure 1.)

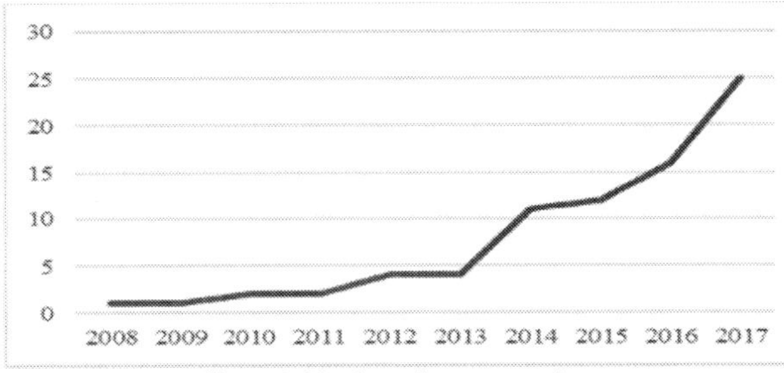

Figure 1. Number of page created per year.

TABLE I. Type of Facebook pages

Type	*Number*
Non-profit organisations (NPO)	7
Websites & blogs	14
Communities	44
Travel agencies, Guides	6
Others (Books, Films, Sports, Events, etc.)	7

Compared to similar religious phenomena like Ladies of Fatima in Portugal or Lourdes devotees in France, the presence of Compostela hikers is significant on Facebook, but compared to the number of francophone hikers, it is not. Less than 1% of the hikers have a Facebook page for the year 2017. We found 25 Facebook pages for 8,835 hikers. These pages have been classified by the creator as shown in Table I.

The Camino de Santiago – the Way of St. James – has always been an identity phenomenon. In the Middle Ages, pilgrims were belonging to various religious brotherhoods, benefiting from their assistance system (such as organization of groups to avoid the high level of insecurity of the ways) or a chapel in the parish church. Communities on Facebook reflect these two dimensions that we can measure by the number of likes in each page. These virtual communities vary between 27,775 for the largest one, which is defined as a community, and 8 persons for the smallest one, which is a Non-Profit Organization (NPO). These figures have been updated on February 15, 2018. The difference could not be explained by the longevity of the page. The oldest one, *RadioCamino* [14], has been created on August 28, 2008 and capitalizes 3 563 likes and the newest one, *Mon chemin à Compostelle* [15] has been created on December 29, 2018, and capitalize 44 likes. The aims of both pages are quite similar. For the largest community, we can read on the *About* section: "All the information to enjoy the experience of Compostela Ways: advantages of each way from France, where to stay, monuments, landscapes…" and the aim of the smallest one is to help those who make the way to Santiago de Compostela in "Touraine". As these figures show, brotherhoods and chapels can also be found on Facebook.

Today motivations have become secularized. NPOs and communities replaced brotherhoods of the past. Interactivity is the magic word. This is done in two ways, by commenting on a post or by posting a message on the page if this function is available. This was the case for 69 pages from the selected corpus and 45 had a response rate higher than 90% that may reflect the desire to share with others. In general, hikers share their feelings, thoughts, progression, experience, photos, video, etc. and the community reacts, reassures or encourages. Sometimes they thank hikers for the shared information. NPOs provide assistance and advice.

Today, social networks have become essential to gather information for Compostela Ways and for sharing information and provide assistance, as the objectives of the pages suggest. Commercial Facebook pages (around 8%) have the same weaknesses as personal pages: contact information is missing and there are not many followers (There are 2,163 followers for the oldest page created in 2012 [16]. The analysis of these pages shows an obvious lack of professionalism: Pages are not very active (less than 30% of interaction), the *About* page is not really enticing. If this weakness is permissible with a personal page, it is less acceptable from a professional one.

To be successful, the communication on FB pages should be optimized in order to increase user engagement. Posting too little or too much information can damage engagement and interaction with followers. The Compostela hikers post less than one message per day except for three pages that have an average of 6.6 [17], 2.7 [18] and 2 [19] posts per day.

Facebook pages is a part of the identity of Compostela hikers. All of them have a Frontpage in accordance with the standards. However, most of them do not depict the full context that helps to engage people, and they do not give information about their identity, even though, trippers leave enough traces to be able to capture some traits of their identity.

The privileged means of communication remains the text, with the photo being widely used as well and the video, but to a lesser extent. Around 50% of the pages do not use photos, and 73% do not use videos.

Many hikers (22%) did not post any information on their pages. Often, the page FB accompanies the walker on his/her journey and dies shortly after the end of the adventure.

Numerous pilgrim walkers exchange on Facebook about preparation or keep in contact after the trip on the Ways. Most of the associations linked to Compostela (Saint-Jean-Pied-de-Port, Pyrenean Piedmont, etc.), as well as the more official institutions (Archbishopric of Compostela) have their own Facebook page, sometimes in several languages. They provide above all information, statistics, advice, addresses. In the past, their forums were not, in our opinion, very interactive; today, with Facebook, this is no longer the case. Nevertheless, this digital dimension of the pilgrimage becomes more and more important, especially the social network.

C. Bourret [1] proposed a typology of the people met on the Compostela Ways that may be extended to users of social networks:

- Authentic pilgrims (with main religious motivations),
- Semi-pilgrims or walkers pilgrims in different groups including those called by Spanish, "turistigrinos", a mix of tourists and pilgrims,
- Hiker-pilgrims, above all for the pleasure of the walk and its interactions,
- Sportsmen or sportswomen, often walkers but also cyclists or riders, in search of physical experience and exceeding their limits.
- Cultural walkers, cyclists or riders very interested by various monuments and cultural heritage,
- Minimalists, only walking a few kilometers to collect the precious stamp on the "credential" to finally obtain the precious "Compostela" as the others.
- Strictly tourists.

There are always different degrees of involvement and participation: from a few days (with special organized trips, particularly in May) to more than 2 months, but almost always in one direction, rarely going back by the same Ways, but using cars, coaches, trains or planes to return home.

VI. Conclusion

For us, interactions, identities and representations on the Compostela Ways are very revealing ambivalences and questionings of all our society.

The proposed paper constitutes a first step of a work in progress.

We always return transformed by our participation in the Compostela Ways and by our interactions with other people but also by finding. In future works, we would like to try to consider the evolution of the representations and the identities of voluntary "pilgrims", at the beginning and at the end of the "pilgrimage" and thus the changes produced by their experience.

The Compostela Ways are a particularly favorable ground for meetings others but also finding oneself, constitutive of the widened "thought," central in the new humanism advocated by L. Ferry [20], who tries to answer the question of the sense of the existence, which is at the heart of the crisis of contemporary individualism.

The Compostela phenomenon is a good way to investigate one's identity, and more specifically the digital identity, with all the traces left on social media. Through the queries of the "trace man", we go back to the eternal question of the meaning of life and of our presence on Earth. Humans do not escape their fate, which is to try to understand (or not) the meaning of their lives, regardless of the communication medium or device they use. The identity and existence questions remain as is.

References

[1] C. Bourret, "Cultural Heritage, Tourism, Identity and Sustainable Development of Territories: the case of the Compostela Ways," in *SGEM Vienna 2017, Conference Proceedings, Book 6 Science and Arts*, Hofburg Congress Center Vienna, Mar. 2017, pp. 3–14.

[2] Oficina del Peregrino [Pilgrims Office] , "Informe estadistico," [Statistical Report], 2016. [Online] Available: https://oficinadelperegrino.com/wp-content/uploads/2016/02/peregrinaciones2016.pdf.

[3] B. Galinon-Mélénec, "L'"Homme trace", arguments," [The trace man, arguments] in L'Homme trace: Perspectives anthropologiques des traces contemporaines [The trace man : Anthropological Perspectives of contemporary traces], B. Galinon-Mélénec, Ed., Paris: CNRS, 2011.

[4] F. Stutzman, "An evaluation of identity-sharing behavior in social network communities," *International Journal of Performance Arts and Digital Media*, vol. 3, no. 1, 2006.

[5] M. A. Smith and P. Kollock, Eds., *Communities in cyberspace*. London, New York: Routledge, 1999.

[6] P. Rateau, P. Moliner, and J.-C. Abric, "Social Representation Theory," *Handbook of Theories of Social Psychology*, 2012, pp. 477–497, 2012.

[7] F. Bernard, "Organiser la communication d'action et d'utilité sociétales. Le paradigme de la communication engageante," [Organize the communication of action and societal usefulness. The paradigm of the engaging communication], *Communication et organisation*, no. 29, pp. 64–83, 2012.

[8] D. Jodelet, "Les représentations sociales: Regard sur la connaissance ordinaire," [The Social Representations: Issue on the ordinary knowledge], *Sciences humaines*, no. 27, pp. 22–24, 1993.

[9] J.-C. Ruano-Borbalan, "La représentation: une notion clef des sciences humaines," [The representation: a key concept of humanities and social sciences], *Sciences humaines*, no. 27, pp. 16–18, 1993.

[10] M. Gauchet, Le désenchantement du monde: Une histoire politique de la religion [The World disenchantment: A Political History of Religion]. Paris: Gallimard, 1985.

[11] P. Breton, L'utopie de la communication: Le mythe du village planétaire [The communication utopia: the myth of the global village]. Paris: Editions La Découverte, 1997.

[12] P. Flichy, "La société de communication," [The communication society], *Cahiers français*, vol. Comprendre la société, no. 326, pp. 65–69, 2005.

[13] P. Nadal, El Camino de Santiago a pie [The Camino de Santiago Walk]. Madrid: El País, 2008.

[14] *RadioCamino: Les chemins vers Compostelle [RadioCamino: ways to Compostela].* [Online] Available: https://www.facebook.com/radiocamino/. Accessed on: Feb. 15 2018.

[15] *Mon chemin à Compostelle [My way to Compostela].* [Online] Available: https://www.facebook.com/m.et.m.compostelle/. Accessed on: Feb. 15 2018.

[16] *Randonnées St Jacques de Compostelle [Hiking Santiago de Compostela].* [Online] Available: https://www.facebook.com/RandonneesCompostelle/. Accessed on: Feb. 15 2018.

[17] *Compostelle 40 [Compostela 40].* [Online] Available: https://www.facebook.com/compostelle40/. Accessed on: Feb. 15 2018.

[18] *Chemin Saint-Jacques de Compostelle (Camino de Santiago) [Way to Santiago de Compostela].* [Online] Available: https://www.facebook.com/CheminSaintJacquesdeCompostelle/. Accessed on: Feb. 15 2018.

[19] *Chemin de Compostelle [Way of Compostela].* [Online] Available: https://www.facebook.com/Chemin-de-Compostelle-801524849973655/.

[20] L. Ferry, *Apprendre à vivre* [Learn to live], Paris: Flammarion, 2015.

M-learning as a Motivational Method in Music Education

Walena de Almeida Marçal Magalhães, Diogo Souza Magalhães, Jônatas Alvarenga Carvalho,
Jefferson José Galvão Monteiro and Cláudio de Castro Monteiro
Federal Institute of Education, Science and Technology, Palmas, Brazil
E-mails: walena@ifto.edu.br, diowalbr@gmail.com, jonatascarvalho@gmail.com,
jephgalvao@gmail.com, ccm@ifto.edu.br

***Abstract* — The use of Information and Communication Technology (ICT) in education is a relevant research topic. With the improvement of technology, the use of mobile phones by students is more and more common in the classroom, enabling an appropriate environment for mobile learning (M-learning) through the 'bring your own device' method (BYOD). Mobility is needed when trying to develop digital media tools. This paper analyzes how art and music students in the context of Brazilian high school technical education can be motivated towards supplementary research through these support technologies in order to build and optimize their own Musical Arts knowledge and skills. The primary objective is to guide teachers in using applications as a tool in the teaching and learning process.**

Keywords - Mobile learning; Technology; Music Education; Art; Education.

I. INTRODUCTION

Recent changes in Brazilian educational rules introduced through Law 11.769/2008 [1] require all Brazilian schools to offer music classes. To overcome the challenges of enhancing Musical Arts and music education, Brazilian Federal Institutions, which are a network of federal technical and technological schools distributed throughout the country, are striving to provide their staff and teachers with specific training in music.

Additional challenges within this context include: a need for innovation in educational resources and methods, better communication with the local art and media production sectors and support for students in their needs as a young generation. Examples include M-Learning, Distance Learning (DL), the use of recent technologies, especially in ICT and their application in M-learning and the promotion of autonomous research, as well as the development of didactic tools and resources.

In consideration of contemporary educational opportunities and challenges, the goal of this paper is to provide guidance and motivation to the Federal Institute of Education, Science and Technology of Tocantins - Palmas Campus, so that teachers and students of Musical Arts may expand the application of technological and didactic tools to improve their skills in information and communication resources for a more effective teaching and learning process.

This paper lays out the process of producing a mobile application using current and publicly available technologies to support the teaching and learning process in Musical Arts, including suggestions for integrating student training within technical education, at the Federal Institute of Tocantins.

An important objective is to make the contents of the subject more attractive to the students and to prompt the students to deepen their Musical Arts knowledge. This involves audio and video examples, exploring technological aspects as supportive and motivational tools for learning the content presented in the classroom, including an engaging theoretical basis, creative exercises to help assimilate contents, and complementary research.

To achieve educational results in the exploratory field of new teaching techniques, the challenges of mobility must be solved, since, without mobility, all the efforts employed in the elaboration of digital media will have been in vain. Considering that the method of access to the didactic contents defined was through BYOD, this required compatibility of a great diversity of devices in order to choose the final tool that was made available to students.

In order to address this subject and report on the experience, this paper is divided into the following parts: in Section II, relevant related work on the topics of mobility and education is presented; in Section III, we discuss the research paper proposal, with specifications of materials and methods; in Section IV, the results of the research are presented, through the analysis of the data collected; in Section V, the results and the possibilities of future work are indicated, highlighting the acute use of technologies relative to youth behavior, as well as the application of the App to other subject areas.

II. RELATED WORK

Magalhães [2] addresses the challenges of Internet use in the present educational context, since the current generation was born in a technological era.

Chen [3] points out that even in Asia, where technology is quite advanced, music teachers have three particular concerns about the use of technology in music classes: equipment setup, technical support, and financial burdens.

After analyzing the use of technology in music education, Silva [4] determined that this subject needs to incorporate an entire set of knowledge to achieve better musical practice, involving various applications for proper relevance to Musical Arts as an area of knowledge.

Ali et al. [5] understand that the benefits of mobile devices include ease of access, storage of information, and mobility for academic and social media.

Franchi and Blanco [6] caution that some Brazilian state laws forbid the use of smartphones. The authors suggest, therefore, that teachers and schools must pay attention to the nearly unlimited possibilities for other uses of technology in musical learning processes. A large variety of technologies can be explored for increasing student skills in working with rhythm patterns, timbre, and other sound properties, since technologies are part of the lives of young people and of how they spend much of their time.

Farley et al. [7] indicate that the use of Apps can provide support and increased knowledge to students both in and out of the classroom. The Apps also allow the teachers access to some excellent complementary educational materials through mobile tools.

Camacho [8] reiterates the importance of motivation as fundamental to the teaching and learning process, emphasizing that students need to develop a positive attitude towards the process. The use of technology in the classroom is essential for motivating development, and aids in student assimilation of musical skills.

Wilmer, Sherman and Shein [9] call researchers' attention to the need for studies that also address how the overuse of mobile devices can affect human behavior.

Regarding the contemporaneity and importance of M-learning within the field of Education, Ally and Prieto-Blázquez [10] posit that this is probably the most important current area of educational research and Sung, Chang and Liu [11] argue that the increase of computing portability and the expanded use of mobile networks (wireless communication) have become powerful sources that merit application within traditional classrooms and beyond, particularly as tools of innovation in education.

III. Proposal

The purpose of this work is to encourage the supplementing of Musical Arts disciplines in high schools, and technical schools with ICT and educational technologies. The intent is to provide students and teachers with technological tools in a way that makes those more attractive platforms to support learning and complementary research processes, and to motivate them in applying those support tools for the efficient and effective learning of the contents presented in the classroom.

This proposal seeks a solution to the challenges of innovation and the incorporation of technology within music education. The specific areas of attention include: encompassed improvement in creative interaction between teacher and students; the awakening of students to a more effective participation in and out of class; the expansion of research in applying technology to the practice of Music; enhancement of the quality of contents given in the classroom; increased engagement of students in the teaching and learning process in Music, and corresponding improvement in interest and attitude; improved interdisciplinarity between Music and other areas of knowledge, starting with IT, providing the impetus for technical education for the productive sector of the local culture and beyond.

This implies a paradigm shift that involves an open environment of collaborative education, since the teacher of the music disciplines will no longer restrict his or her approach to classroom teaching merely to traditional contents, such as paper and pen, magnetic board, computer to multimedia projector, group dynamics, classroom socialization and other teaching methodologies. While those approaches may still be relevant, the teacher and students will also use mobile devices and networks; favoring this kind of environment in the educative context, enables greater interactivity with students, which can motivate them to deepen their musical knowledge, through research, assimilation exercises and artistic creativity. This will help, since "in this fast-changing world, different stakeholders will have to work together to develop new educational models to cater for new generations of learners who will be using mobile technologies that do not exist as yet." [10] (p.145).

This paper results from the need to confront learning problems presented by the current generation of adolescents, herein referred to as the "youth generation", who from the first decade of life have had contact with contemporary technologies and media, as well as the future generation, which is already considered the "virtual generation". It is clear that educational institutions and professionals have the challenge of producing more collaborative content, as well as learning to apply it through virtual environments, which incorporate technology in the classroom and innovate in pedagogical practices.

A. *Materials*

This research was developed in the graduate course in Telematics. The research group work consisted of joint meetings at the computer science laboratory of the Federal Institute of Tocantins, alternating with virtual meetings each week.

Since the course uses the Problem Based Learning (PBL) methodology, the first part of each meeting was dedicated to solving problems that were presented to the research group by a tutor. This involved rational deliberation, particularly focused on how the various portions of the project would be carried out. The second part of the meetings was devoted to searching for solutions to proposed issues. Virtual meetings made use of cloud-available tools such as BigBlueButton [12], Youtube [13], WhatsApp [14], Gmail [15], Google Family - Classroom [16], Drive [17], Hangouts [18], Docs [19], Sheets [20], Slides [21], Forms [22] - and Overleaf [23].

In order to provide students and teachers with technological tools to support the teaching and learning process, much of the research was devoted to creating an App capable of applying content related to Musical Arts subjects in digital formats available in the cloud and accessible through mobile devices, such as smartphones, tablets, computers (desktops and notebooks) and other kinds of media with an Internet browser. It was necessary to develop an application compatible with various smartphone platform operational systems, currently used for centralization of the content and ordering in a didactic form defined by the teacher of the discipline.

A variety of functionalities were created in the application to enable its use in or out of the class [6], such as quiz resolution. The digital contents formed by texts, images and videos were presented by the teacher in the classroom and accompanied by students through their own smartphones. On occasion, when students did not have access to their smartphones in class, they were allowed to work with a partner (see Figure 1).

Figure 1. Students working in pairs to appreciate musical examples.

Quizzes, texts and complimentary videos were attached so that students could use them by themselves outside of class (see Figure 2).

Figure 2. Student using Ritornello App in Art/Music class.

To develop the application, the following items were used: computers (Itautec desktop and Dell and Samsung notebooks) with Linux and Windows operating systems, with broadband Internet access, a Publisher type subscription of the AppSheet [24] tool to provide the system, Google Drive [17] for digital content storage (PDF, Images, etc.), YouTube [13] for video sharing, Google Sheets [20] to manipulate the content offered in the application, and the following smartphone devices for testing: Asus Zenfone 3, Iphone 5, Iphone 7 and Samsung Galaxy J5 Prime.

To carry out the experiment in the classroom, a raspberry (a hardware computer of the size of a credit card) was available via the G-Redes Group; a Wi-Fi network board and a patch cord ("short" network cable) were used to provide Internet access broadband to students for their own devices to interact with the content applied by the teacher [6]. This router (see Figure 3), called "Tadeu", had software that was appropriately constructed and integrated to its functioning by another research group linked to Federal Institute, called Network Applied Research Group (NARG). The software gains are: (1) Wi-Fi signal flashing, (2) optimized management of user connections, (3) continuity of roving user connections and (4) stability.

The device and its operating program were created to promote better network signal capture and reception. It is a Wi-Fi router, equipment with two standard 802.11 Wi-Fi interfaces and a 100Mb Ethernet interface, with a system developed by the research group applied to computer networks on the Palmas Campus, which allows seamless and autonomous access to the Internet, using a wireless connection.

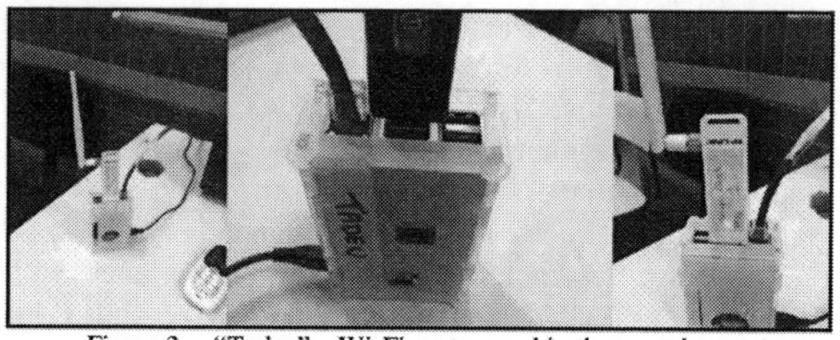

Figure 3. "Tadeu" – Wi-Fi router used in the experiment.

This Wi-Fi mobility is the fundamental basis for everyone to have Internet access through their own device. During the experiment, Internet access was offered through the institute's own data network, as detailed in the previous paragraph; however, access through other means of communication such as LTE, 3G, 4G among others, were enabled. In the version of the application used in the experiment, the content that most required data bandwidth were the videos, which require, as specified by YouTube, a stable connection of at least 1 Mbps so the students could watch the contents without interruptions.

The experiment was repeated 9 times with different classes (see Figure 4) of approximately 25 students. At the end of each class, the students were asked to submit an evaluation questionnaire with questions regarding the teaching tool and how well it met the students' satisfaction for use with the new technology applications.

Figure 4. Experiment in an IT class technical course – Middle School

To achieve a satisfactory result, it was established that the reliability coefficient for the research would be at least

95%. To reach this level of reliability, it was necessary to define the minimum sample size. Considering that the size of the selected population (students of the Musical Arts discipline) was 160 persons, a total of 115 individuals were asked to answer the questions. The equation to arrive at this result is described in (1), which is called *sample*:

$$a = \left(\frac{\gamma x\ 1{,}96}{\varepsilon}\right)^2 \qquad (1)$$

Where:
a = sample
γ = standard deviation
1, 96 = trust level
ε= estimated error

The collection of the research was done through a *Google Forms* electronic form at the end of each class through the application itself - *Ritornello* App - which was developed during the research.

After data collection, the results were tabulated for each question, indicating the percentage marked for each alternative and the calculations of standard deviation and the sample error, reaching the variance as in (2):

$$S^2 = \Sigma\left(\frac{Xi - X}{n-1}\right) \qquad (2)$$

Where:
S^2 = variance
Σ = sum
Xi = value of element
X = average of elements
n = number of elements

At the end, the standard deviation of each item was calculated to obtain the standard deviation as described in (3):

$$S = \sqrt{\ } S^2 \qquad (3)$$

Where:
S = standard deviation
S^2 = variance

With the tabulated results, a joint study was carried out for debugging the values and understanding the final result, which will be explained in more detail in the subsequent section.

B. Methodology

This research is action research "characterized as a type of research based on empirical research, designed and in close association with the resolution of a collective problem, in which researchers and participants are involved in a cooperative manner." [25] (p. 163 - translated by the authors).

IV. Results

In order to optimize Musical Arts learning through the efficient and effective use of information and communication resources, the conclusion is that it is essential for the education area to keep up with innovations in technology and communication in order to reach students in the contemporary world with its challenges and the new culture that presents itself.

To do this, research is needed for the development and use of new technology applications and implementation of tools that accompany this process of contextualizing education to the new times. Expositive classes, magnetic frames with brushes and group dynamics, for example, can and should be used, but other resources need to be added to the educational dynamics, since educators working in elementary through high school education are dealing with a generation born within the digital age and exposed to it as early as the first decade of life.

The results of this research were obtained through the interpretation of data collected by an evaluation questionnaire developed in Google Forms and applied at the end of each class, when all the students could answer through the App Ritornello itself, after the presentation of the contents scheduled for that class. A total of 115 questionnaires were filled out, with 10 multiple choice questions in each questionnaire (see Table 1), each one with 5 options, with the student selecting only one option for each question.

The questions involved topics such as the coherence between the contents of the Ritornello platform and the teaching plan of the Music Arts discipline, their facilitative and complementary nature, the effectiveness of the evaluations of the contents given in class, through the quizzes in the App, frequency of the App use by the students outside of class and about the user experience, encouragement of academic motivation and degree of educator-student interaction, navigability and the influence of the App on student's artistic creativity.

TABLE I. RITORNELLO EVALUATION QUESTIONS

NR	Questions
1	Is the organization in the *Ritornello* platform coherent with the teaching plan of content in the Musical Arts course?
2	Did *Ritornello* help you learn the Music Arts content better?
3	How much did the contents of *Ritornello* help to complement your knowledge of the discipline?
4	How efficient were the quizzes in evaluating your learning of the contents?
5	How often did you use or think you will use the App outside of the classroom?
6	How satisfied are you with *Ritornello* App in comparison with traditional classes?
7	Did *Ritornello* make you more interested in the Arts / Music discipline?

8	How would you rate the teacher-student interaction with the usage of *Ritornello*?
9	How easy is it to handle the *Ritornello* App?
10	Rate how the App influenced the development of your creativity and artistic expression?

All the questions were answered immediately after use of the App with the intent of showing its effectiveness and to point to improvements for future work.

A. *Data Analysis*

Question 1 (see Figure 5) dealt with the organization of contents on the App *Ritornello* platform, observing its coherence in relation to the teaching plan of the Music Arts subject.

The results were that 43.5% (50 students) of respondents perceived great coherence between the contents and the platform, 31.3% (36 students) perceived enormous coherence and 25.2% (29 students) saw coherence between the two. The standard deviation of this question is 17.36%, with a sampling error of 3.17%. Thus, 100% of those who answered understand that there is a very positive relationship between the content taught in the course and the application platform, which certainly favored and strengthened the learning of the presented contents.

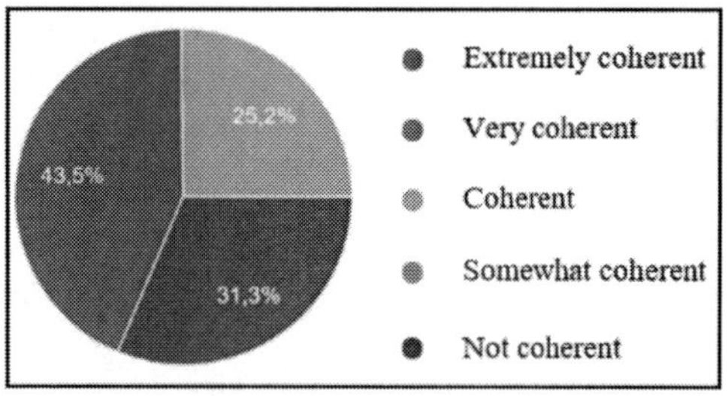

Figure 5. Question 1 results.

Question 2 (see Figure 6) evaluated the effectiveness of *Ritornello*. For this item, 35.7% (41 students) of respondents answered that App *Ritornello* was a good help for learning the content better, 33% (38 students) answered that it helped a lot, 28.7% (33 students) answered that it helped. It was observed that 97.4% (112 students) of the responses were positive, pointing to the application as a tool that facilitates the educational process. Only 2.6% (3 students) evaluated the contribution as being of "little help". The standard deviation of question 2 is 15.45%, with a sampling error of 2.82%.

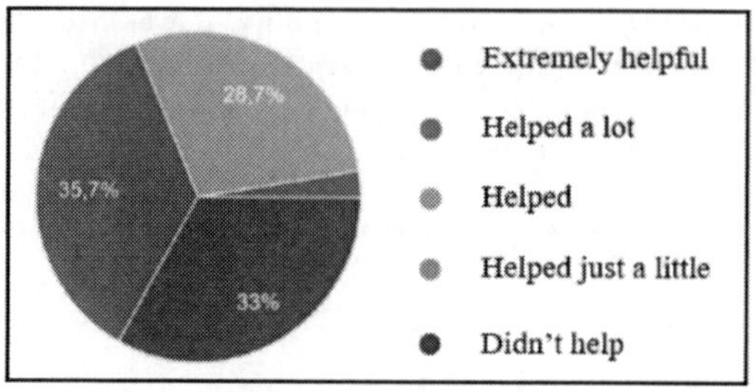

Figure 6. Question 2 results.

In Question 3, the purpose was to test the App's complementary character in relation to the course contents. More than half of the students, 57.4% (66 students), said that the App greatly complements the contents of the music subject ("a lot"), 21.7% (25 students) answered that the App complements extremely the music contents and 20% (23 students) said that it complements moderately ("Reasonably"). In resume, 99.1% (114 students) believed that the App fulfills well the role of complementing the educational process in the classroom. Only 0.9% (1 student) considered the complementary character of the App invalid ("Nothing") (see Figure 7). The standard deviation of this question is 20.82%, with a sampling error of 3.80%.

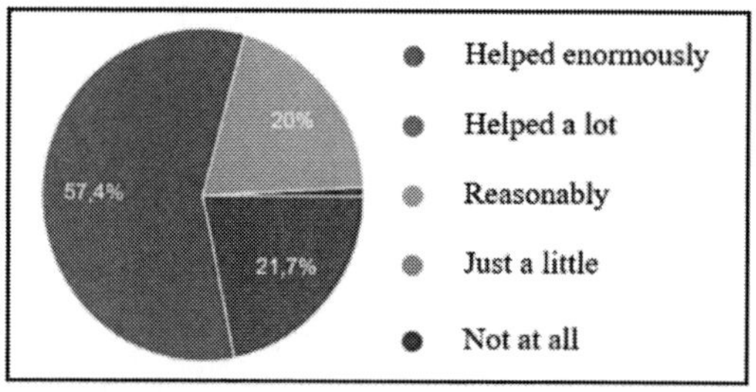

Figure 7. Question 3 results.

Question 4 relates to the quizzes in the App and their effectiveness in evaluating contents. In the answers (see Figure 8), 39.1% (45 students) believe that the quizzes evaluated very well, 31.3% (36 students) said that they evaluated well and 25.2% (29 students) evaluated them as an excellent tool for evaluation. Thus, 95.6% (110 students) acknowledged that the quizzes fulfilled their role of efficiently evaluating the learning of contents per unit, favoring the pedagogical process. In this question, only 4.3% (5 students) concluded that this evaluation was fair. No one considered the quizzes to be inadequate. The standard deviation of this question is 15.27%, with a sampling error of 2.79%.

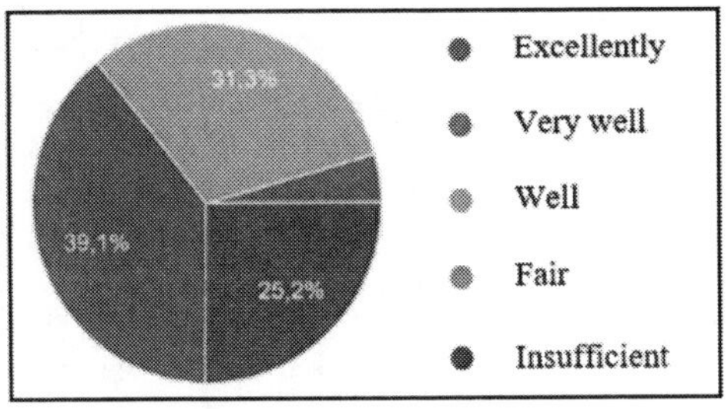

Figure 8. Question 4 results.

In Question 5, the focus was on how often the students would use the App outside the classroom. The answers (see Figure 9) showed that 48.7% (56 students) reported that they were able to use the App only once a week, 23.5% (27 students) were able to use it twice a week, 13% (15 students) once a day, 9.6% (11 students) never used the App outside of the classroom and 5.2% (6 students) were able to use it 2 or more times a day. With this, 72.2% (83 students) agree that *Ritornello* is a complementary technology tool to be used in or out of class to deepen the contents of the discipline. Despite this, 27.8% (32 students) of those who answered the questionnaire evidenced using the App at other times and places, which may greatly extend the application function in the future. The standard deviation of Question 5 is 15.56%, with a sampling error of 2.84%.

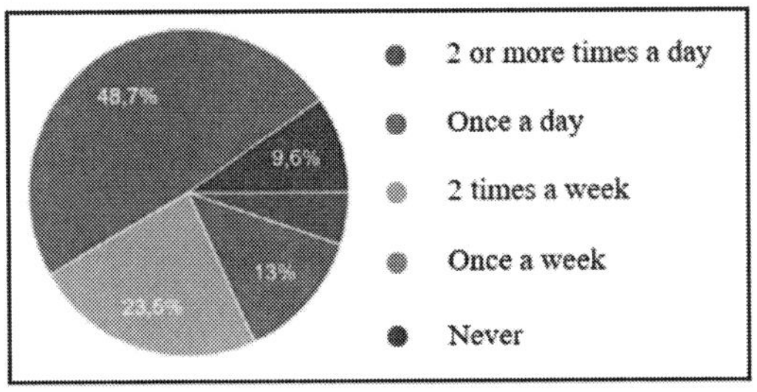

Figure 9. Question 5 results.

Question 6 evaluated the degree of acceptability of users with the use of the App in relation to traditional classes (see Figure 10), 49.6% (57 students) of the evaluators stated that they are pleased with the App, 35.7% (41 students) said they were greatly pleased, 12.2% (14 students) felt that their use was indifferent in relation to traditional classes, 7% (2 students) reported being slightly pleased and 0.9% (1 student) expressed displeased. In total, 85.3% (98 students) of the students showed acceptance of the use of the App in its relation with traditional classes, evidencing that it presents a positive differential, and is able to potentialize the educational process. The standard deviation of this question is 19.39%, with a sampling error of 3.54%.

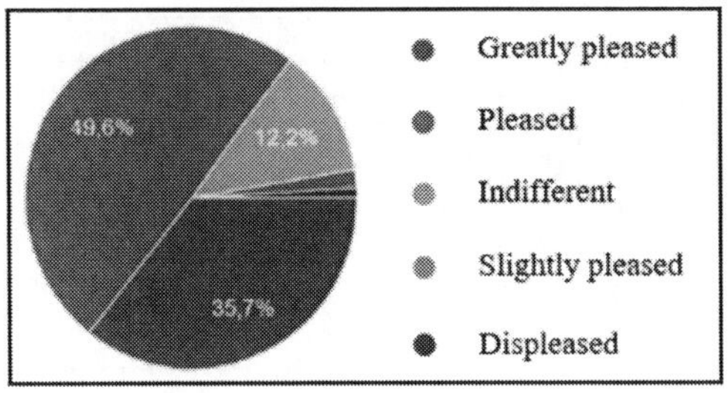

Figure 10. Question 6 results.

Question 7 inquired whether the use of the Ritornello App increased the student's interest in the Music Arts discipline (see Figure 11). 46.1% (53 students) of the respondents said yes, they were a little more interested, 32.2% (37 students) answered yes, they were much more interest, 13% (15 students) said that it was indifferent, 7.8% (9 students) pointed that they continued having the same interest and 0.9% (1 student) that their interest has decreased. Only 0.9% (1 student) affirmed that interest in the subject decreased due to its use and 20.8% (24 students) evidenced that they were not affected by the interest in the discipline by using the App. The standard deviation of Question 7 is 16.68%, with a sampling error of 3.04%.

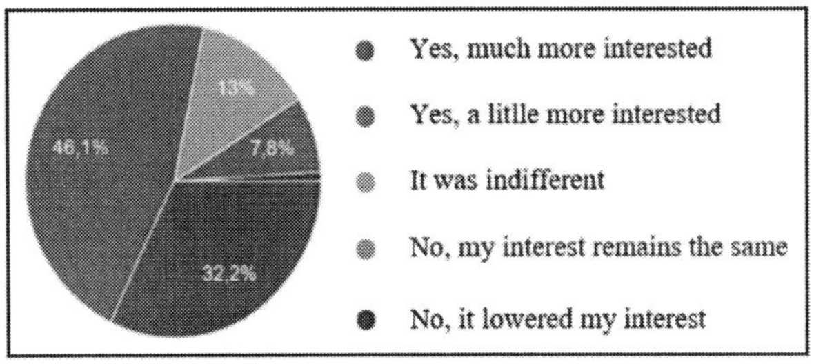

Figure 11. Question 7 results.

Question 8 measured the student-educator interaction. More than half of the respondents, 51.3% (59 students), said that the interaction improved, 34.8% (40 students) that the interaction improved a lot, 13.9% (16 students) answered it was indifferent and 86.1% (99 students) believed that there was an increase of interaction between teacher and students through the use of *Ritornello*. No one said that using the App made it difficult to interact or said that its use eliminated the interaction. The standard deviation for question 8 is 20.18%, with a sampling error of 3.68%. Contrary to what might be commonly thought, the research results point to a positive relationship between actors in the educational process by the use of new technologies in the classroom (see Figure 12).

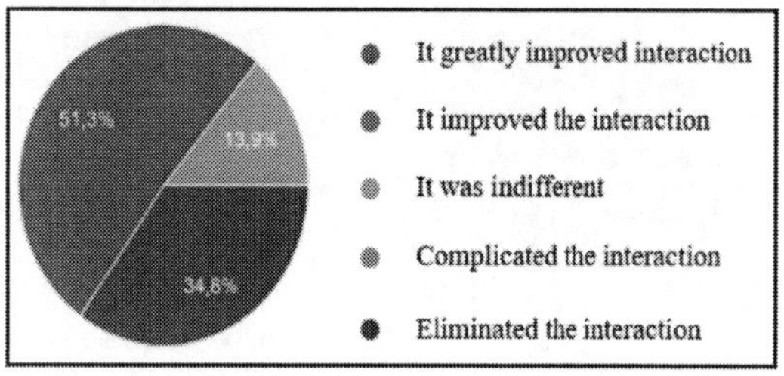

Figure 12. Question 8 results.

Question 9 evaluated the degree of usability of the App. 34.8% (40 students) of respondents said that the use is very easy, 30.4% (36 students) said that is relatively easy and 31.3% (35 students) found it easy. From the respondents 96.5% (111 students) believe that *Ritornello* App is user-friendly. Only 3.5% (4 students) stated that it was difficult to use the application. The standard deviation of this question is 15.02%, with a sampling error of 2.74%. With this response, it is possible to say that *Ritornello* can be widely used in high school and even adapted for use in lower education, to younger people and people who are not accustomed to the use of technologies (see Figure 13).

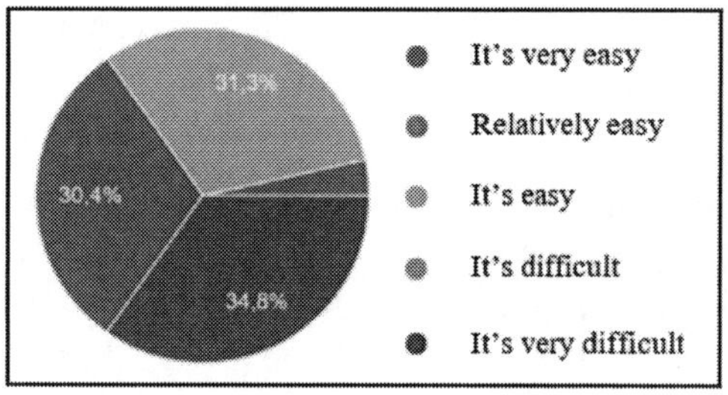

Figure 13. Question 9 results.

Question 10 evaluated the relation between the use of *Ritornello* and the increase of students' creativity ability and its application in students' artistic expression. More than half, 57.4% (66 students), said that the App helped a lot in such development and 20% (23 students) answered that it helped very much, making a total of 77.4% (89 students) holding a positive opinion. Additionally, 18.3% (21 students) were indifferent, 2.6% (3 students) believed that the App did not help with creative subjects and 1.7% (2 students) said that it was of little help in such development. The standard deviation of question 10 is 20.18%, with a sampling error of 3.68% (see Figure 14).

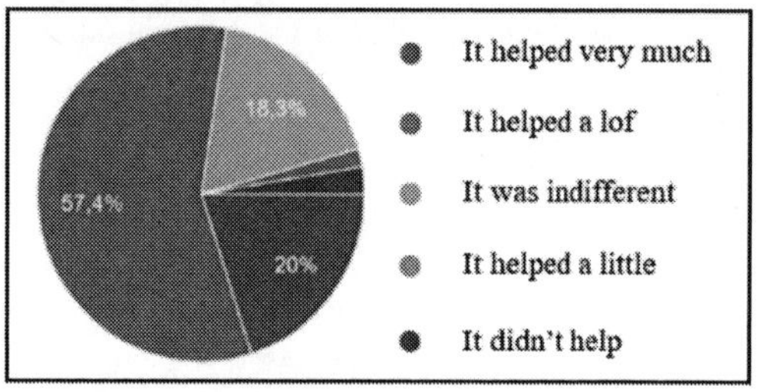

Figure 14. Question 10 results. [red] It was a good help

V. Conclusion And Future Work

Technology has much to contribute to education, as has been demonstrated by the use of television, multimedia devices and computers for some decades in the classroom. However, the most recent technologies, such as smartphones, also merit application to education, particularly in the context of a hyper-modern world where a large proportion of the population already has access to a portable high-tech device.

Music education, as with other areas of knowledge, needs incentives and adjustments, with properly trained teachers, appropriate methodologies and didactic materials, and updated pedagogical tools that stimulate learning at all levels of the educational system.

The *Ritornello* App was able to supply some of these needs through increased student engagement, which resulted in higher interest in Musical Arts studies, as well as an enhanced teaching and learning process that provided greater satisfaction to the actors involved in it.

Nevertheless, some challenges persist: the lack of broad or consistent access to technology in Brazilian schools; the need for better continuing education training for teachers in the use of technologies; more complete and adequate access to personal computers by students; and of course, the development of more technological educational tools.

Further research will be needed concerning the implementation and monitoring of these tools in the classroom so that they can provide the results appropriate to the environment for which they were created.

Beyond that, it is possible to research how Ritornello could be applied with a broader spectrum of subject and content areas. Based upon the data collection performed in the user experience (UX), the application can undergo further adaptations and improvements. Its relevance could be expanded to various disciplines and contexts of education, capitalizing on its powerful pedagogical potential for dramatic expansion of formal education.

Additional tools could be developed to provide the teacher with further classroom App support; for example, it would be useful to develop a tool which might provide the teacher with graphs to accompany each student's access number, indicating their progress toward learning goals, completion of exercises, and levels of achievement.

As for the development of tools to aid in teaching (M-Learning), it is possible to conclude that the mobility factor should be considered as a premise, given the need to meet the requirements of availability in multiple platforms and the great diversity of devices and means of communications existing at present. The use of specific features of mobile devices such as smartphones and tablets, with devices such as: Camera, Microphone, Accelerometer, Gyroscope, Magnetometer, GPS and others, can be explored in future work to obtain new user experiences.

Another aspect that merits further study is the impact that acute and extensive use of technology may have on student cognition and behavior, especially regarding effects on relationships, social interactions, and long-term physical and mental health care and relational aspects, since there is a dynamic correlation between Education, Technology and Communication. Given the virtually unlimited potential of these tools, innovative investment and expansion is highly promising, but should be carried out with due caution and appropriate diligence.

REFERENCES

[1] Brazil. "Federal Law nr. 11.769 from Aug 18th, 2008," in: Official Diary of the Federative Republic of Brazil, Brasília, DF, Ago 19th. 2008, pp. 1. Available from: <http://www.planalto.gov.br/ccivil_03/_ato2007-2010/2008/lei/l11769.htm>. Accessed: 2018.03.10.

[2] W. M. Magalhães, "The challenges of Internet use for higher education research," in: Evangelical Praxis, vol. 20. FTSA: Londrina/Brazil, 2012, pp. 121-129.

[3] C. W. J. Chen. "Mobile learning in music education." The Oxford Handbook of Technology and Music Education. Edited by S. Alex Ruthmann and Roger Mantie, 2018, pp.1-10. Available from: <https://www.researchgate.net/publication/322592634_Mobile_Learning_in_Music_Education>. Accessed: 2018.04.23.

[4] N. M. da Silva, "Integration of new technologies into the educational process of specialized music teaching," Aveiro University, 2016, pp. 1-102. Available from: <http://ria.ua.pt/bitstream/10773/17687/1/Disserta%C3%A7%C3%A3o%20Mestrado%20final.pdf>. Accessed: 2018.03.25.

[5] G. Ali, B. P. Mbabazi, N. Lawrence, and A. Geoffrey. "Use of mobile devices by students to support learning in universities: a case of Muni University." 2017, pp.69-80. Available from: <https://www.researchgate.net/publication/318129220_use_fo_mobile_devices_by_students_to_support_learning_in_universities_a_case_of_muni_university>. Accessed: 2018.04.27.

[6] L. E. Franchi and S. M. Blanco, "Mobile phones in the music class: use of cell phones with 8th grade students of a public school in Belém - Pará - Brazil," in: IX ABEM North Regional Meeting. UFRR, 2016, pp. 1-14. Available from: <http://abemeducacaomusical.com.br/conferencias/index.php/ixencontroregnt/reg_norte2016/paper/viewFile/1574/767>. Accessed: 2018.05.01.

[7] H. Farley et al., "How do students use their mobile devices to support learning? A case study from an Australian Regional University" 2015 Journal of Interactive Media in Education, 2015(1): 14, pp. 1–13. Available from: <https://jime.open.ac.uk/articles/10.5334/jime.ar/>. Accessed: 2018.04.21.

[8] C. de P. Camacho, "Technological tools and motivation for learning," master's degree dissertation. University Fernando Pessoa, Porto, Portugal, 2017, pp. 1-122. Available from: <http://bdigital.ufp.pt/bitstreeam/10284/6042/3/DM_Carmen_Camacho.pdf>. Accessed: 2018.02.20.

[9] H. H. Wilmer, L. E. Sherman, and J. M. Chein. "Smartphones and cognition: a review of research exploring the links between mobile technology habits and cognitive functioning." in: Frontiers in Psychology 8, 2017: 605. *PMC*. <https://www.ncbi.nlm.nih.gov/pmc/articles/PMC5403814/>. Accessed: 2018.04.24.

[10] M. Ally and J. Prieto-Blázquez, "What is the future of mobile learning in education?" in: University Magazine and Knowledge Society (RUSC), vol. 11, n. 1, 2015, pp. 142-151. Available from: <https://link.springer.com/content/pdf/10.7238%2Frusc.v11i1.2033.pdf>. Accessed: 2018.03.10.

[11] Y. Sung, K. Chang, and T. Liu. "The effects of integrating mobile devices with teaching and learning on students' learning performance: A meta-analysis and research synthesis". In: Computers & Education, Vol 94, March 2016, pp. 252-275. Available from: <https://www.sciencedirect.com/science/article/pii/S0360131515300804>. Accessed: 2018.04.21.

[12] BigBlueButton, Available from: <https://bigbluebutton.org/>. Accessed: 2018.06.03.

[13] Youtube, Available from: <https://youtube.com>. Accessed: 2018.06.07.

[14] WhatsApp, Available from: <https://www.whatsapp.com>. Accessed: 2018.06.02.

[15] Google Gmail, Available from: <https://www.google.com/gmail/>. Accessed: 2018.06.08.

[16] Google Classroom, Available from: <https://classroom.google.com>. Accessed: 2018.06.07.

[17] Google Drive, Available from: <https://www.google.com/drive/>. Accessed: 2018.06.09.

[18] Google Hangouts, Available from: <https://hangouts.google.com/>. Accessed: 2018.06.07.

[19] Google Docs, Available from: <https://www.google.com/docs/about/>. Accessed: 2018.06.04.

[20] Google Sheets, Available from: <https://www.google.com/sheets/about/>. Accessed: 2018.06.07.

[21] Google Slides, Available from: <https://www.google.com/slides/about/>. Accessed: 2018.06.09.

[22] Google Forms, Available from: <https://www.google.com/forms/about/>. Accessed: 2018.06.05.

[23] Overleaf, Available from: <https://www.overleaf.com/>. Accessed: 2018.06.07.

[24] Appsheet, Available from: <https://www.appsheet.com/>. Accessed: 2018.06.06.

[25] B. D. Schmitt and J. C. Medeiros, "Action research: directing the production of scientific articles in the area of physical education and health," in: Journal of the Department of Physical Education and Health and the Master in Health Promotion of the University of Santa Cruz do Sul/ Unisc. Year 15, vol. 15, n. 3 - July/September, 2014, pp. 1-5. Available from: <https://online.unisc.br/seer/index.php/cinergis/article/viewFile/5171/3898>. Accessed: 2018.05.09.

Fast Extraction of Statistically Relevant Descriptor Words for Social Media Communities

Arnulfo Azcarraga
[1] Software Technology Dept
College of Computer Studies
De La Salle University
Manila, Philippines
arnie.azcarraga@delasalle.ph

Arces Talavera[1, 2]
[2] Dept of Computer Science
and Information Engineering
National Taiwan University of
Science and Technology
Taipei, Taiwan
arces_talavera@dlsu.edu.ph

***Abstract*—Social media communities can be characterized by descriptor words that are frequently used by its community members but are less often used in other communities. These can be extracted by computing a descriptor index and choosing those words with the highest index. The novel descriptor index proposed here is based on the z-score that measures the frequency of a word in a given community relative to the frequency of the word in all the communities combined, using a statistical standard error. The measure based on z-scores is validated by comparing the words extracted when using z-scores with the words extracted using the fairly popular Term Frequency-Inverse Document Frequency (TF-IDF) and the Lagus method. Once it is established that z-scores can be used to extract descriptor words, the next hurdle is to reduce the dimensionality of the vector space model, where each word that appears in any of the social community messages would constitute one dimension in the vector space model. The solution explored here, used in tandem with z-scores as descriptor index measure, is the Random Projection method. In this dimensionality reduction method, more than 40,000 unique words (dimensions) are randomly projected to as few as 400 dimensions (99% reduction) and yet the proposed scheme still extracts essentially the same descriptor words for each community. To evaluate the combined use of z-scores and Random Projection, and to determine some suitable parameter values for the proper execution of the Random Projection method, 10 communities on Facebook were selected. Despite using only 1% of the original number of dimensions, there is a match of 85% of the top 10 descriptor words between those extracted with all 40,000 dimensions compared to those extracted with only 400.**

Keywords*—*Random Projection; Dimensionality Reduction; Social Media; Text Analytics.

I. INTRODUCTION

The emergence of social media allowed the users of the Internet to share their own content and information with others, and to have the opportunity to form their own virtual social network [1]. In fact, social media users are drawn together and are more likely to connect and participate in a social network having people who are popular or people who are similar to them, such as other users who prefer to use the same language as them [2][3].

Characterizing communities in social media networks using descriptor words that are frequently used by the community members is useful when one needs to quickly distinguish one community from another. This can be done by computing a descriptor index measure for each word, and choosing the top k words with the best descriptor index measures.

The descriptor index proposed here is based on the z-score that measures the relative frequency of a word in a given community, with a confidence interval, from the frequency of the word in all the communities combined, using a standardized computation of the statistical standard error. The measure based on z-scores is validated by comparing the words extracted when using z-scores with the words extracted using Term Frequency-Inverse Document Frequency (TF-IDF) [4] and the Lagus method based on a goodness measure [5]. Such descriptor words are very useful in Text Mining [6], as well as in other more focused application areas, such as human and social analytics. One simply considers the descriptor words to have a fairly good idea of what the given social media community is concerned with.

Text mining for all its vast potential, however, faces the challenge of having to deal with very large volumes of documents. This in turn translates into a very high dimensional vector space model – where each word that appears in any of the social community documents/messages would constitute one dimension in the vector space. The high dimensionality elevates both the computational and space complexities [7] of any task involving the unique words and phrases that appear in the documents. Indeed, even if we can establish that z-scores can be used to extract descriptor words, the next challenge is to drastically reduce the dimensionality of the vector space model.

Dimensionality reduction is understandably a widely researched area in text mining [7] and other areas, such as image processing, bioinformatics, and so on [8][9]. One method stands out. The Random Projection method [10] randomly projects the high-dimensional features of a dataset into a far smaller low-dimensional space, to as little as just 1% of the original dimensionality of the vector space. And yet, when properly used in combination with other algorithms that are compatible with the projection method, the performance of the low dimensional space is comparable to that in the original, high-dimensional space.

The rest of the paper is organized as follows. Section II describes the characterization of social media communities with a novel bag-of-words representation using z-scores, and validates the proposed approach by comparing the extracted descriptor words to those extracted by TF-IDF and the Lagus method. Section III illustrates how the Random Projection method works, and how it can be used in combination with the z-scores that are computed as descriptor index. Section IV contains the discussion of the experimental results that are designed to fine-tune the parameter values of the Random Projection method. The paper ends with Section V, which contains the conclusions.

II. Characterization of Social Media Communities Using Z-Score

Online social networking applications nowadays implement a "verified user system" to emphasize the importance of opinion leaders, such as celebrities having numerous followers [11]. These leaders are able to make use of the "public reach" provided to them by the social networking site in order to gain lots of attentions and to promote their products and services to their followers.

Every social network community formed by a celebrity and his/her followers often gravitate towards a small subset of words, sometimes transforming to a veritable "jargon", that over time would be good descriptor words that would characterize the interest, motivation, and even the socio-cultural and linguistic characteristics of the community as a whole.

For the rest of the discussions and experiments in this paper, we use a huge collection of individual "posts" published as public comments on the Facebook pages of 10 well-known Filipino celebrities, having hundreds of thousands or even millions of followers. These posts were collected using Facebook's Graph Application Programming Interface (API) [12].

The steps of preprocessing the dataset include the removal of non-alphanumeric characters, digits, and unnecessary white spaces. In addition, both Filipino [13] and English [14] standard "stop words" in the posts are removed. The remaining tokens/words are then stored using a bag-of-words representation in a vector space. This resulted in a large celebrity dataset containing 40,126 words, where each unique word is considered as an individual "feature".

A. Z-score

The z-scores of each of the words of each of the communities are then computed as their "descriptor index", and the top k words with the highest z-scores in each community are considered to be the descriptor words.

The z-score of a word can be calculated using the following formula:

$$z = \frac{p-P}{SE_P} \tag{1}$$

where p is the proportion of the usage of the word relative to all the words in the same community, while P is the proportion of the usage of the word relative to all the words in the corpus (in this case, all 10 communities). SE_P represents the standard error of the word in the population. This is computed using the following formula:

$$SE_P = \sqrt{\frac{P(1-P)}{n}} \tag{2}$$

where n is the number of words in the given community.

Note that the z-score is very commonly used in statistics to test whether the proportion in a given sample is no different from the "ideal" proportion, in this case the population proportion. Candidate descriptor words of a community have proportion p that is significantly larger compared to P (proportion in all the communities combined).

To test the plausibility of using z-score in extracting the descriptor words of a community, we compute these scores for each word in each of the 10 communities and we extract the top 10 descriptor words. These are shown in Figure 1 as word clouds. Note that the communities have different descriptor words, and when taken together, they give a good idea of the type of discussions that happen in each community. For example, the celebrity "Mocha Uson" has "Duterte (current president of the Philippines)", "pangulo (president)" and "bayan" (country) as descriptor words. Indeed, she was an active endorser of President Duterte on social media since the campaign period in late 2015. The socio-linguistic characteristics of the celebrities are also apparent. Lea Salonga, Erwan Heussaff, and Anne Curtis have posts that are mostly in English, while the others are mostly in Tagalog. One of the known local celebrities who is known to often be talking of her son has the nickname of her son as one of the extracted descriptor words. Another female celebrity has the name of her husband, also a local celebrity, among the descriptor words.

Fig. 1. Top 10 descriptor words for every celebrity, whose names are written in red text, if z-score is used as the measure to characterize each community.

Note that descriptor words need not be unique to a given community. However, when descriptor words are far too common, and appear as descriptor in almost all communities, then they are no longer suitable descriptor words. From Figure 1, we note that using the z-scores kept two terms *po* and *thank*, which are tagged as descriptor words for two celebrity communities. This can be caused by the 2 communities having an extraordinarily high proportion of usage of the terms – such as the Tagalog speakers who use the "po" (as a sign of politeness) in almost every sentence.

B. TF-IDF

TF-IDF is the function commonly used to measure the importance of the terms in a given document [15]. This is a standard metric in the vector space model for text mining where the best terms to represent a document are those with high Term Frequency (TF) but at the same time should also be rarely used in other documents - high Inverse Document Frequency (IDF).

In a way, TF alone can be used to extract the descriptor words of a community. It is the proportion of the occurrences of a given term to the entirety of the terms in a given community. The formula for computing TF is as follows:

$$TF_{i,j} = \frac{n_{i,j}}{N_j} \tag{3}$$

where $n_{i,j}$ would be the number of occurrences of term i in document j and N_j represents the totality of the terms in document j.

The suitability of TF as index to extract the descriptor words of the communities is also evaluated. Using TF as the measure in finding the descriptor words of a community is only partially able to achieve its goal. More words, such as *thank, good, si, po, day,* and *watch,* are extracted for a multiple number of communities. This means that TF alone is not able to truly extract descriptor words when we also require that the ideal descriptor words are common in a given community, but relatively less common in the other communities.

IDF [16] is thus introduced to favor terms that are concentrated only in a few documents/communities. This measure ranges from 0, which represents the words that occurred in the entire corpus, to 1, which represents the words that occurred only in one document/community of the entire corpus. The formula for computing IDF is as follows:

$$IDF_i = \log(\frac{D}{d_i}) \tag{4}$$

where D is the total number of documents in the corpus and d_i is the number of documents using the term i.

Given the nature of IDF, it cannot be used as a lone measure to obtain the descriptor words for a community, but it can be applied to retrieve the words that are common in the corpus, or the words that only occur in a handful of communities.

Combining the weights of both the TF and IDF into the TF-IDF measure would indeed improve the extraction of the descriptor words of a document as it combines the importance of the words inside a specific community, and the exceptional words in the 10 communities (entire corpus). Using the TF-IDF removes the terms that are too commonly used, such as *day, thank, love, today, tonight*, and the like, and some of the very common Filipino stop words that are not covered in the stop word list, such as *po, natin, yung, lang*, and such.

C. *Goodness Measure*

The Lagus method, based on a measure of goodness, describes yet another descriptor word index [5]. It can be observed by ranking the words used in the communities based on the following criteria that: (1) the given word should be more prominent in a community compared to the other words in the same community, and (2) the given word is relatively more prominent in the specified community in the rest of the corpus. The formula for computing the goodness of a characteristic word w given document/community j is as follows [17]:

$$G(w,j) = \mathrm{F_j}(w)\frac{F_j(w)}{\sum_i F_i(w)} \tag{5}$$

where $F_j(w)$ is the proportion of the term w and all the terms in community j. $F_j(w)/\sum_i F_i(w)$ compares the importance of the word w in community j with its importance in the corpus.

D. *Comparison of Results*

Using the z-score as descriptor index measure can be validated by comparing it to other probability-based measures such as TF, TF-IDF or the Lagus method. A large intersection among the top 10 words when z-score is used as the measure and the top 10 words when the other measures are used would indicate that z-scores are also effective for determining the descriptor index measure of words. The intersections for the communities of each of the chosen celebrities are shown in Table I.

TABLE I. INTERSECTION OF THE TOP 10 WORDS WHEN Z-SCORE IS USED AND THE TOP 10 WORDS WHEN OTHER MEASURES ARE USED

Celebrity Community	*TF*	*TF-IDF*	*Goodness*
Anne Curtis	5	4	8
Chito Miranda	6	3	9
Erwan Heussaff	8	2	8
Kris Aquino	7	6	9
Lea Salonga	3	5	8
Marian Rivera	8	6	9
Mocha Uson	7	4	8
Sarah Geronimo	8	5	7
Vice Ganda	9	5	7
Wil Dasovich	8	5	6
AVERAGE	6.9	4.5	7.9

Using the z-score as the measure to find the descriptor words of the communities yields an average of 7.9 out of the top 10 words when compared to using the Lagus method, and averages of 6.9 and 4.5 when compared to TF and IDF, respectively. Much like when evaluating alternative methods that recognize specific objects from images [18][19] (which just need to list the correct object somewhere within the top 5 predicted objects in an image), we do not require that the top descriptor word in each community, that are extracted using z-scores, would be the same descriptor words extracted when using TF, TF-IDF and the Lagus method. Since there is no real "ground truth" as to which are the real top 10 descriptor words, we would simply need to see that there is some fair amount of intersection among the extracted descriptor words when compared to the other methods.

We also compare the results yielded when using TF to TF-IDF and the goodness measure (Table II). Compared to using z-scores, TF is only able to get an average of 2.9 out of the top 10 words when compared to the TF-IDF measure, and an average of 5.6 out of the top 10 words for the goodness measure. Lastly, we evaluate the Lagus method by comparing it to the TF-IDF measure in extracting the top descriptive words of the celebrities. The results are also presented in Table II.

TABLE II. INTERSECTION OF THE TOP 10 WORDS BETWEEN THE VARIOUS PROBABILITY-BASED MEASURES

Celebrity Community	*TF vs. TF-IDF*	*TF vs. Goodness*	*Goodness vs. TF-IDF*
Anne Curtis	2	3	6
Chito Miranda	1	6	4
Erwan Heussaff	1	7	3
Kris Aquino	4	6	7
Lea Salonga	0	2	7
Marian Rivera	5	8	6
Mocha Uson	2	5	6
Sarah Geronimo	5	7	6
Vice Ganda	5	7	7
Wil Dasovich	4	5	7
AVERAGE	2.9	5.6	5.9

The goodness measure of the Lagus method can extract an average of 5.9 out of the top 10 words when compared to the TF-IDF, which has a similar performance as the z-score. Overall, with all the comparisons made, the statistical capabilities of the z-score measure in extracting the descriptive words of the celebrity communities make it a suitable descriptor index measure.

III. Application of Random Projection

The general idea of Random Projection [10] is to project the large number of dimensions of a text corpus (in this case, the single vector space for the 10 social communities) into a much smaller vector space with the number of features being a very small fraction of the original number. Random Projection, as depicted in (6),

$$D(i,j) \rightarrow D'(i,m) \qquad (6)$$

transforms vector space D having i documents (messages/communities), and j unique words each of which is a dimension in D, into vector space D' having the same i documents (communities), and m features, where $m << j$.

The projection takes two parameters, m and r. The first parameter m is the (much smaller) number of features of D', and r represents the number of times a given word (feature) is mapped into any of the m dimensions in the projected space D'.

Random projection uses a j x m projection matrix, where every feature in D corresponds to a row in R. The m columns are the components that act as the new features found in D', such that each column in $D'$is in fact the sum of frequencies of a very large number of randomly selected words. Each word in turn is randomly mapped by R to r different columns in D'. At r = 5 or more, there is a small chance that two unique words would have been mapped by R to exactly the same 5 columns in D'.

Constructing the projection matrix R consists of randomly selecting r unique dimensions in m for each of the j words. A value of 1 is given to each of the r selected components, while all remaining $m - r$ dimensions of row j are set to 0. The values for every document/community in D are computed as follows:

$$d'[f_1 \ldots f_m] = d[f_1 \ldots f_j] * \begin{bmatrix} R_{11} & \cdots & R_{1m} \\ \vdots & \ddots & \\ R_{j1} & & R_{jm} \end{bmatrix}^T \qquad (7)$$

where d' is the resultant, compressed vector in D' for each document d in D.

This Random Projection method thus yields a highly compressed and compact dataset, where each dimension encodes the frequencies of a very large number of words. Note that by the nature of Random Projection, it is not straightforward to choose from m dimensions those that might point us to the suitable set of descriptor words. And, since each of the m dimensions would have mixed up the term frequencies of thousands of words, Random Projection would not be compatible with approaches such as the TF-IDF, which relies heavily on the "rarity" of occurrence of candidate words in documents/communities other than the one for which a descriptor word is being searched.

In the rest of this paper, we go back to z-scores and demonstrate that it is feasible to use it in combination with the Random Projection method – and thus benefit from the ability of the latter to significantly lower the number of dimensions and improve on the time and space complexity of the over-all approach.

Since a z-score relies heavily on the TF except that it also incorporates a test for statistically significant differences in proportions between candidate words, we now show how z-scores can still be used to select descriptor words, even if we drastically reduce the dimensions of our vector space.

All the words in the original dataset are first given the projected z-score value based on the summation of the z-scores of the components in D' where they are projected. As an example, given that the word f_1 is projected into the components m_0, m_3, m_5, and m_{10}, then w is given the value of the summation of the z-scores of the stated components. The process, as shown in Figure 2, is done for all words in the original dataset.

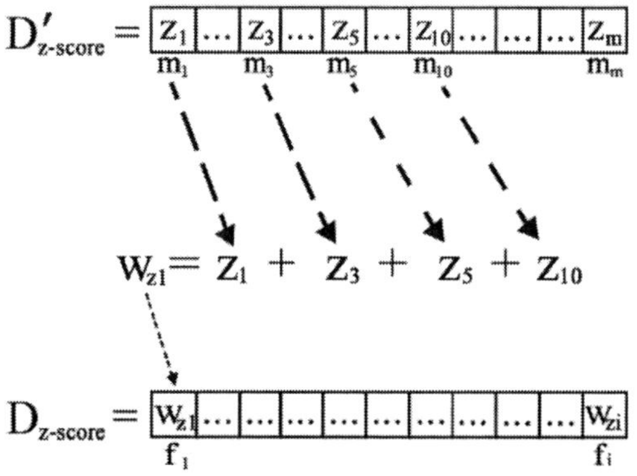

Fig. 2. Process of computing the projected z-score, w_{z1}, of the candidate descriptor word f_1. The z-scores z_1, z_3, z_5, and z_{10} of the components where f_1 is projected are added to determine its projected z-score.

IV. Random Projection Based on Z-Scores

A. Filtering of Riders

Because of how Random Projection works, we can expect that certain words can be mistakenly selected as a descriptor word simply because in the projection they happen to be mapped to the same dimensions where the real descriptor words get mapped to as well. These words are what we call *riders* - that piggy-back on the real descriptor words and thus get high scores for themselves.

Removing such *riders* turns out to be straightforward. We simply apply the Random Projection k times, and words that do not get consistently high scores are plain *riders*. The final scores of the words are computed by taking the average of their projected scores in all of the k trials.

A maximum of 15 Random Projection trials are performed to test if the performance is affected by the number of trials done. Parameter values for the projection matrix used are m = 400 and r = 10. The performance is measured by the number of words that are extracted using only m dimensions that match those extracted words when using all 40,000 dimensions and the comparison is presented in Table III.

TABLE III. Comparison of the performances of the various number of times Random Projection is applied in getting the top words of the non-projected dataset

Number of Trials	*Top 5 Words*	*Top 10 Words*
1	66%	43%
2	76%	68%
3	80%	76%
4	76%	75%
5	80%	84%
6	82%	85%
7	80%	85%
8	82%	86%
9	82%	87%
10	82%	88%
11	84%	88%
12	84%	87%
13	82%	88%
14	84%	89%
15	82%	88%

Performing Random Projection twice already significantly improves its performance from 66% to 76% among top 5 words, and 43% to 68% among top 10 words, when compared to only having done Random Projection once. This shows that the *riders* are easily removed. And, as the number of trials increases, the performance rate of Random Projection improves further. From 9 trials onwards, the performance rate stabilizes between 82% to 84% when taking the top 5 words, while for taking the top 10 words, performance is between 87% to 89%. Since we would not want to make more trials (runs) than what is necessary, we just use 10 trials for the remaining experiments that needed to be conducted to further fine-tune the method.

B. Improving Random Projection Results

We proceed to further improve the performance of the approach by encoding the z-scores before they are accumulated during Random Projection, such as taking the $\log_{10}$ value, its square root, or by squaring it. Taking the $\log_{10}$ or the square root of the z-scores tends to diminish the differences among z-scores, while taking the squared-value would obviously increase the effect of the differences among z-scores (which are mostly numbers greater than 1.0).

In the following experiments, both m and r parameters of Random Projection are given the same old values of 400 and 10, respectively. To evaluate the performance of the techniques applied, we again use the intersection of the top 5 and top 10 descriptor words using the raw non-projected z-scores (all 40,000 dimensions are used) and the projected raw or encoded z-scores. The comparison of performances for the different measures applied is shown in Table IV.

TABLE IV. Comparison of the performances of the various encodings of the z-scores used as the basis

Z-Score Representation	*Top 5 Words*	*Top 10 Words*
raw z	56%	33%
$\log_{10} z$	62%	38%
$\sqrt{z}$	66%	43%
z^2	63%	19%

Indeed, adding encoding to the z-scores has a noticeable effect on the performance of Random Projection. The baseline performance rate of using the raw z-score is 56% when getting the top 5 words, and 33% when getting the top 10 words. Table IV shows that the performance worsens when we use the squared values of the z-scores. Upon inspection, we noticed that, what happened in face was that, when we square the z-scores, the *riders* increase in rank and get selected. Indeed, squaring the z-scores yielded a performance rate of only 36% when taking the top 5 words, and 19% for the top 10 words.

Table IV also shows that, when we diminish the importance of the differences among z-scores by getting the $\log_{10}$ or their square root values, we see an improvement in the performance rate of Random Projection. Using $\log_{10}$ yields performance rates of 62% and 38% when getting the top 5, and 10 words, respectively. Taking the square root of the z-scores has the best performance rates of 66% for the top 5 words, and 43% for the top 10 words.

The performance rates can be even further improved. To fully utilize the capabilities of Random Projection, the next step is to try to find good values for the two parameters: r, the number of times the features will be projected, and m, the number of features of the projected, reduced dataset.

Various combinations of the two parameters, m and r are evaluated. The values of m start with 100, which is then doubled until the value reaches 3,200 (roughly 8% of the original number of dimensions). For r, the experiments start with a value of 5. In this paper, we only show the results for r having values 5, 10, 20, 40, and 80.

This time, 10 trials of Random Projection are done (to remove the riders) and the square root representation of the z-scores are used, at a fixed value of $m = 400$. The comparison of the performances of the different values of r is shown in Table V.

TABLE V. COMPARISON OF THE PERFORMANCES OF THE VARIOUS VALUES OF THE *R* PARAMETER OF RANDOM PROJECTION

Value of r	*Top 5 Words*	*Top 10 Words*
5	84%	85%
10	82%	88%
20	80%	86%
40	74%	85%
80	84%	85%

From Table V, it can be observed that parameter r can be set to low values of 10, or even 5, and yet, good results of over 80% can be achieved. We are left with now finding the value of m, which was set to 400 in the experiments earlier.

The final experiment evaluates the performance of Random Projection when the m parameter is given differing values. For the remaining experiments, 10 trials and square root encoding are used, with the r parameter set to 5. The comparison of the performance rates is shown in Table VI.

TABLE VI. COMPARISON OF THE PERFORMANCES OF THE VARIOUS VALUES OF THE *M* PARAMETER OF RANDOM PROJECTION

Value of m	*Top 5 Words*	*Top 10 Words*
100	80%	71%
200	86%	79%
400	84%	85%
800	76%	88%
1600	88%	91%
3200	90%	94%

As the value of m increases, the performance rate of Random Projection also understandably improves. But since the aim of dimensionality reduction is to get good results in significantly less amount of time, we would prefer lower values for m. At $m = 3{,}200$, the performance rate is 90% when taking the top 5 descriptor words, and 94% when taking the top 10 words. Dramatically reducing the number of dimensions to even just 10% of its original size, at $m = 400$, Random Projection still yields a decent performance of 84% and 85% when taking the top 5 and top 10 descriptor words, respectively.

V. CONCLUSION AND FUTURE WORK

The computation of a descriptor index to extract the descriptor words that characterize social media communities can indeed be based on the z-score that measures the relative frequency of a word in a given community compared to its frequency in all the communities combined.

This novel measure is validated using a collection of "posts" published by 10 well-known Filipino celebrities on their Facebook pages. The words extracted using the z-scores are compared with the words extracted using the TF, TF-IDF, and the Lagus method based on the goodness measure to establish that z-scores can be effective as basis for extracting descriptor words.

The other challenge addressed in this paper is the reduction of the dimensionality of the vector space using the Random Projection method. This dimensionality reduction method randomly projects more than 40,000 unique words to as few as 400 dimensions. This method is used alongside the z-scores as descriptor index measure to accurately and efficiently extract descriptor words for each community.

The combination of z-scores and Random Projection is evaluated using the celebrity dataset. Reducing the dimensionality of the original 40,000 dimensions to only 8% of it (3,200 dimensions) yields a 94% match among top 10 descriptor words compared to using all 40,000 dimensions. Pushing the dimensionality reduction further, using only 1% of the original number of dimensions produces a match of 85% of the top 10 descriptor words compared to those extracted using all 40,000 dimensions. For further benchmarking and validation of the approach, future experiments may concentrate on even larger social media communities, preferably those using English, Spanish, or French, so that a larger comparison and evaluation among alternative techniques may be conducted.

REFERENCES

[1] P. M. Napoli, "Social media and the public interest: Governance of news platforms in the realm of individual and algorithmic gatekeepers," *Telecommunications Policy*, vol. 39, no. 9, 2015, pp. 751 – 760.

[2] P. Saha and R. Menezes, "A language-centric study of twitter connectivity," in *Social Informatics*, E. Spiro and Y.-Y. Ahn, Eds. Cham: Springer International Publishing, 2016, pp. 485–499.

[3] P. Saha, *Language relations on twitter: A network science approach*. PhD [Dissertation]. Melbourne, FL: Florida Tech., April 2017. [Online]. Available: http://hdl.handle.net/11141/1417 [Retrieved April 2018].

[4] G. Salton and C. T. Yu, "On the construction of effective vocabularies for information retrieval," in *Proceedings of the 1973 Meeting on Programming Languages and Information Retrieval*, ser. SIGPLAN '73. New York, NY, USA: ACM, 1973, pp. 48–60.

[5] K. Lagus and S. Kaski, "Keyword selection method for characterizing text document maps," in *Proceedings of the 1999 International Conference on Artificial Neural Networks*. IET, 1999, pp. 371–376.

[6] Y. Zhang, M. Chen and L. Liu, "A review on text mining," in *2015 6th IEEE International Conference on Software Engineering and Service Science (ICSESS)*, Sept 2015, pp. 681-685.

[7] G. S. Reddy, "Dimensionality reduction approach for high dimensional text documents," in *2016 International Conference on Engineer & MIS (ICEMIS)*, Sept 2016, pp. 1-6.

[8] W. Awada, T. M. Khoshgoftaar, D. Dittman, R. Wald and A. Napolitano, "A review of the stability of feature selection techniques for bioinformatics data," in *2012 IEEE 13th International Conference on Information Reuse & Integration (IRI)*, Las Vegas, NV, 2012, pp. 356-363. doi: 10.1109/IRI.2012.6303031

[9] D. L. Padmaja and B. Vishnuvardhan, "Comparative study of feature subset selection methods for dimensionality reduction on scientific data," in *2016 IEEE 6th International Conference on Advanced Computing (IACC)*, Feb 2016, pp. 31–34.

[10] C. H. Papadimitriou, H. Tamaki, P. Raghavan, and S. Vempala, "Latent semantic indexing: A probabilistic analysis," in *Proceedings of the Seventeenth ACM SIGACT-SIGMOD-SIGART Symposium on Principles of Database Systems*, ser. PODS '98. New York, NY, USA: ACM, 1998, pp. 159–168.

[11] W. X. Zhao, J. Liu, Y. He, C. Y. Lin, and J. R. Wen, "A computational approach to measuring the correlation between expertise and social

media influence for celebrities on microblogs," in *2014 IEEE/ACM International Conference on Advances in Social Networks Analysis and Mining (ASONAM 2014)*, Aug 2014, pp. 460–463.

[12] Facebook. The graph api. [Online]. Available: https://developers.facebook.com/docs/graph-api/ [Retrieved Nov. 2017].

[13] G. Diaz. Stopwords iso. [Online]. Available: https://github.com/stopwords-iso/stopwords-tl/blob/master/stopwords-tl.txt [Retrieved Nov. 2017].

[14] University of Glasgow. Stop word list. [Online]. Available: http: //ir.dcs.gla.ac.uk/resources/linguistic utils/stop words [Retrieved Nov. 2017].

[15] G. Salton and C. Buckley, "Term-weighting approaches in automatic text retrieval," *Inf. Process. Manage.*, vol. 24, no. 5, pp. 513–523, Aug. 1988.

[16] K. Sparck Jones, "Document retrieval systems," P. Willett, Ed. London, UK, UK: Taylor Graham Publishing, 1988, ch. A Statistical Interpretation of Term Specificity and Its Application in Retrieval, pp. 132–142.

[17] K. Lagus, S. Kaski, and T. Kohonen, "Mining massive document collections by the websom method," *Inf. Sci.*, vol. 163, no. 1-3, pp. 135–156, Jun. 2004.

[18] A. Krizhevsky, I. Sutskever, and G. E. Hinton, "Imagenet classification with deep convolutional neural networks," in Advances in neural information processing systems, 2012, pp. 1097–1105.

[19] K. Simonyan and A. Zisserman, "Very deep convolutional networks for large-scale image recognition," arXiv preprint arXiv:1409.1556, 2014.

Toward "Satisficing" Creativity Effort within Project Management

Leonie Hallo
Entrepreneurship, Commercialisation and Innovation Centre
The University of Adelaide
South Australia 5005, Australia
e-mail: leonie.hallo@adelaide.edu.au

Alex Gorod
Entrepreneurship, Commercialisation and Innovation Centre
The University of Adelaide
South Australia 5005, Australia
e-mail: alex.gorod@adelaide.edu.au

Anama Morriss
Entrepreneurship, Commercialisation and Innovation Centre
The University of Adelaide
South Australia 5005, Australia
e-mail: anama.morriss@adelaide.edu.au

Abstract— **Project management plays an important role in our society as most work activities are organized around projects. While many are successful, a large number of projects fail due to the inability to meet project management constraints. One of the key constraints is that of budget, and projects often go over the planned budget. This happens because of inefficient allocation of resources to such critical areas as fostering a culture of innovation and creativity. It is a current standard practice to maximize creativity regardless of the nature of the project. However, such an approach is not always effective, and this paper proposes an adaptive decision-making framework based on the degree of project complexity. The framework can be used to determine the "satisficing" level of creativity effort needed to be generated and supported depending on the project type. In turn, this can lead to a more productive allocation of resources and achievement of project goals.**

Keywords-optimizing; satisficing; creativity; project management; project complexity

I. INTRODUCTION

Projects often go over budget with significant negative consequences for the project concerned [1]. This is partly due to the waste associated with ineffective use of resources: and part of this is the extensive expenditure allocated to fostering creativity. Fostering creativity requires significant investment [2]. Although creativity is crucial, fundamental and at the center of innovation, all of the effort and cost expended on creativity must be financially accountable. Is there a point where additional resources devoted to creativity effort produce less and less return on investment, and if so how is that point determined? Even though creativity is important and needed, there may be times when investments in creativity effort may be greater than the project warrants. This paper presents a method of assessing whether investments in creativity efforts are appropriate and justifiable. The complexity of a project is a factor which needs to be considered when making an investment in creativity. What this paper is proposing is that the investment in creativity needs to be matched with the complexity of the project; that is, how much creativity effort is warranted needs to be assessed against the level of complexity of the project. This assessment will result in more effective investments in creativity.

It is generally believed that creativity is always positive, and that fostering creativity is always a good investment [3]. Typically, decision-makers tend to optimize or maximize creativity in an effort to obtain the best result for a given project. In general, project management is based upon the concept of optimization. However this is not always the best way to go, especially under conditions of severe constraints [4]. It has become standard practice to maximize expenditure on creativity, regardless of the nature of the project. However, such an important project management decision should be financially accountable. This paper focuses on decision-making: in particular, the decision whether or not to invest additional resources into creative solutions to a project. This type of decision-making occurs in social human analytics, and the benefit of this approach is that it recognizes that investing more resources will not necessarily lead to better outcomes.

The paper analyses investment in creativity against the effectiveness of that investment as it relates to the complexity of the project and proposes a framework which can be useful in helping project managers to determine the most effective allocation of resources invested in creativity effort under differing levels of complexity. Investing in the right amount of creativity will be cost-effective: fostering too much creativity for the project is costly; on the other hand, insufficient creativity effort will also be costly in terms of loss of opportunity. It is therefore important that the project manager assesses the complexity involved in the project of interest before investing in creativity effort. The paper addresses a way of assessing a project and its degree of uncertainty, and then applying the correct level of creativity to match that project. The framework will assist project management decision-making regarding how much to invest in creativity effort, and this will mean greater efficiencies. The framework minimizes the loss or waste associated with unused creativity effort.

Section II of this paper discusses the benefits and costs of creativity efforts; Section III looks at an approach to allocating creativity efforts; Section IV presents a typology of projects based on degree of complexity; Section V discusses benchmarking creativity in line with project complexity; Section VI presents a model; and Section VII concludes the paper.

II. Benefits and Costs of Creativity Efforts

There are many ways to define creativity and there is no one universally accepted definition, but creativity is generally viewed as entailing the production of something novel and appropriate [5]. Other definitions focus upon usefulness and aesthetics [6]. Howard et al. [7] listed several keywords describing creativity, including unobvious, adaptive, unexpected, resourceful. Creativity is therefore considered to be about producing outcomes which are different from expectations or from the norm. The relationship between individual creativity and organizational innovation has been investigated [8], as has the optimal method for organizations to encourage creativity in the working environment [9]. Creativity has also been linked with resilience [10], through for instance the capacity of flexibility. Metzl and Morrell [10] suggest that creativity can be a predictor as well as a facilitator of resilience. Creativity clearly has many benefits.

Creativity can be considered solely as a mental process of the individual: however, some authors contend that creativity is also social and cultural. Social systems make judgements about the creative products of individuals and decide whether and how valuable they are. A systemic approach assesses creativity against various interacting systems. For example, the evolving systems approach of Gruber (1988) considers three interacting systems, which through their interaction make the creative work; knowledge, purpose and affect. A systemic approach to creativity, then, asserts that the cognitive process occurs within a context and that looking at the process itself and not considering the importance of the context is a limited view of creativity. The creative person is interacting with the environment and those interactions affect the internal process of creativity. Csikszentmihalyi [11] proposed the DFI model of creativity which contains three major component systems; the domain, the field and the individual. The system of the field consists of people who make the judgements about what is creative and valuable and what is not. The creative process is thus considered to be not just the emergence of an idea, but also considers the larger process in which that idea is impactful and accepted. Ideas need to be used to be useful. A systemic approach addresses not just whether a creative idea is generated but also the extent to which an idea has an impact in its field and is accepted as a creative contribution in that field. There is a larger process beyond the creative act itself.

Within the realm of project management, creativity is the engine of innovation: without creativity new ideas do not evolve: and innovation is necessary for businesses to maintain competitiveness. Improved processes, new markets, new products all arise as a result of creative thinking, and companies need to foster creativity in order to maintain their competitive advantage. However, there are costs involved in encouraging creativity in terms of investments in money, time, resources, staff and leadership; and the investment in creativity efforts needs to be justifiable.

III. An Approach to the Allocation of Creativity Efforts

There are multiple approaches to the allocation of creativity efforts. One of the standard approaches is optimization. Project managers often choose this as their decision-making method, but there are limitations to this approach. Optimizing or rational decision-making consists of exploring all the available alternatives and then choosing the best possible option to achieve the best outcome. In using this approach, the project manager decision-maker needs to have a full knowledge and understanding of all the creative possibilities and options and must be able to assess those possibilities in an effective way. However, there are problems with this method of allocating creativity effort. Because in the real complex world rationality is bounded due to various constraints, it is not always possible or feasible to make an optimizing decision about the deployment of creativity and to encourage maximum creativity effort by considering all the options.

An alternative approach to optimizing is that of "satisficing" [10]: this approach is more adaptive to the complexity of a project. Projects are becoming more and more complex and require a different form of decision-making than optimizing. High-quality decision-making under complex conditions has spawned a number of tools such as decision trees, probability analysis, Monte Carlo simulation and others [12]. "Satisficing" is one decision-making method for complex projects and involves searching through the available alternatives until an acceptability threshold is met. "Satisficing" is a decision process used when all the available alternatives cannot be feasibly listed out and the best alternative chosen in an orderly fashion. If the project is dynamic, there are unclear boundaries and emergence is occurring, it is necessary instead to choose a "satisficing" "good enough" option which will satisfy a previously set benchmark [13][14]. Within project management, a "satisficing" decision will mean not continuing to invest in creativity efforts beyond the point when that investment will not be effective.

This paper suggests that, traditionally, project managers tend to optimize creativity, irrelevant of the degree of complexity. When a project is simple, it is feasible to optimize. However, when a project is complex, it is not feasible, and "satisficing" is what will be required. This paper suggests that it is necessary to decide whether it is appropriate to optimize creativity or instead use "satisficing", so that investments can be more effective. In this way, creativity efforts will only be engaged when they are really needed.

IV. A Typology of Projects Based on the Degree of Complexity

The degree of complexity present within projects varies: not all projects are the same based upon the variable of complexity. Several different typologies of project complexity have been proposed: this paper is based upon the typology of Snowden and Boone [15], which presents a model of four levels of complexity, similar to the work of Volberda [16]. This framework has been applied across many domains including medicine [17]. Quantification of complexity is still in the early stages [18]. In this typology, projects are recognized as falling into four main types, as listed below;

A. Simple

Known; in simple projects, operations are predictable and repeatable; cause and effect are clear. There is no need for analysis or experimentation as the outcomes are known. This is the area of knowable best practice.

B. *Complicated*

Known unknown; in the case of complicated projects, there is some degree of interconnectedness of constituents and problems are those of coordination or specialized expertise. Cause and effect can be surfaced through analysis. Investigation, analysis and specialized knowledge are helpful in this kind of scenario. Good practice, not best practice, is applicable to complicated problems.

C. Complex

Unknown unknown; in complex projects, it is not possible to know and understand all the features within any project and there are ambiguity, unpredictability and uncertainty: because of the dynamic nature of the project, things are constantly changing, and emergence occurs. The management process is about probing, identifying possible responses, trial and error and evaluation. This scenario is not about imposing best practice or good practice, but rather emergent practice. Previously established protocols are not likely to work in complex projects. Cause and effect are understood only in retrospect.

D. Chaotic

In chaotic projects there is high turbulence and constant change, and there are no clear cause and effect relationships. The project is very dynamic and flexible and produces a lot of outcomes. The boundary of the system is not clearly definable. A great amount of information is flowing around in the system and the project manager needs to make sense of this information and propose a clear way forward. Decisions need to be made quickly and there is no time for consultation; communication is top-down. Establishing a focus and a sense of control may be more important for managers than selecting the 'right' or best way to respond. Gaining control is the first imperative [15].

V. Benchmarking the Level of Creativity in Line with the Complexity of the Project

Traditionally, the complexity of a project is not considered when assessing how much creativity effort should be fostered; rather, decision-makers tend to maximize creativity efforts under all conditions. However, this paper suggests that complexity is important in making the decision about the level of creative effort to be deployed. There are benefits and costs for creativity in each type of context, as presented below.

A. Simple Project

1) Benefits of creativity

Even in simple projects, some people need the stimulation of varying their approach to keep their mind on their work and to avoid being bored, which can lead to carelessness and a loss of focus [19].

2) Costs of creativity

In simple projects, creativity may impede work progress [20]. The scenario is known and understood and there is not much need for creativity effort. When the instructions are clear, and the task is straightforward, it is more efficient and accurate for people to follow the rules as they are laid out. Deviations from instructions are unnecessary and may be damaging and wasteful. Organizations do not need a great amount of creativity in the simple project.

B. Complicated project

1) Benefits of creativity

In complicated projects, there is room for minor adjustment in ways of approaching a problem to get an optimal outcome. Complicated projects often require the input of experts [15]. A moderate amount of creativity will be useful under these circumstances.

2) *Costs of creativity*

Whenever experts need to be brought in, this cost will need to be built into the assessment of the investment.

C. Complex Project

1) Benefits of creativity

In complex projects when things are changing rapidly, there is much more uncertainty and it is necessary to encourage as many ideas as possible, to use a trial and error approach to address unique, fast changing project challenges. This is the field for a high level of creativity effort and innovation. Enabling leadership which encourages creative effort is important [21][22]. There may be a paucity of resources, including time. There is no blueprint for how to respond and there is a need for ideas generated specifically for the project [23].

2) Costs of creativity

As well as considering the costs of wide consultation with a variety of participants, if a great number of creative ideas are produced, many of them can be wasted, especially if management has no control [17].

D. Chaotic project

1) Benefits of creativity

In a chaotic project there are opportunities for innovations, provided the project can be managed. Decision-making in the chaotic project is not straightforward. The project manager needs to decide how to channel decisions to the correct level of decision-making: some decisions are simple and not requiring creativity; some decisions will be complicated and there may be room for some creativity; some decisions will be complex and require a great deal of creativity. The decision to act may be simple, but the process of execution will require some creativity in how resources are organized and applied [23]. In the chaotic project, maximum creativity effort is useful.

2) Costs of creativity

There is often a lack of control and it is possible that creativity effort will be wasted. In a chaotic project, all ideas generated may not able to be capitalized upon because there is no boundary of the system. Too much creativity effort is destructive and distracting because people can lose sight of their objectives. If there is limited time to reach a solution the fostering of an excessive amount of creativity effort will cause a loss of focus.

VI. Creativity and project complexity: A model

Not all projects require high levels of creativity. Figure 1 shows that optimizing in simple projects is unnecessary. There are not many outcomes and there is not much built-in uncertainty: there is no need for a range of different approaches and investment in creativity is unnecessary. As projects become more complex, more uncertainty is present, and a wider variety of approaches and solutions is needed. To deal with this variety of outcomes, a commensurate variety of approaches is needed. Ashby [24, 25] indicated in his Law of Requisite Variety that the variety of solutions available within a project must be at least equal to the variety of problems which need to be addressed. Thus, a complex project needs sufficient creativity and innovation in devising a variety of approaches to match the complexity contained within the project. In a chaotic project, maximum creativity effort is needed to cope with the turbulent environment. Thus, optimization of creativity effort is beneficial. However, it is difficult to capitalize on all the ideas generated and there will be a lot of waste.

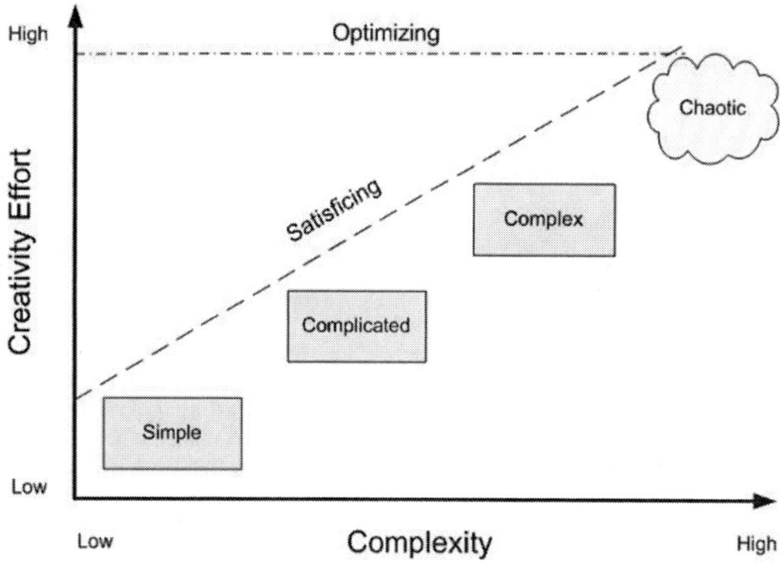

Figure 1. The relationship between complexity of the project and creativity effort

When "satisficing" is undertaken, the right amount of ideas is generated, and waste is minimized. Choosing to optimize under all circumstances without considering the complexity of the task is clearly an inefficient approach and an incorrect investment into fostering creativity [26]. The framework shown in Figure 1 is useful because project managers need to assess the type of project they are dealing with before deciding the amount of creativity effort which is needed: and this consideration will lead to greater investment effectiveness overall.

As an example, consider the following scenarios as an illustration of decision-making at various levels of complexity. The project is to transform an uninhabitable piece of land into a livable solution. At the simplest level, a person may go to a dealer of mobile homes to make their selection. There may be limited options available, the person chooses one, and arranges for delivery. There is no customization, no preparations are needed, and the mobile home is already complete. Creativity effort is not necessary. Alternatively, the person may decide to use a partly customizable dwelling in the form of a modular home. They go to a dealer who has five different modules which can be assembled in various combinations. Now, there are more outcomes and the decision scenario entails a greater amount of choice. The home is complete but does need foundations and sewerage and other considerations concerning the environment. Some creativity effort will be needed. At the more complex level, a person may decide to commission an architect to produce detailed plans for a highly customized unique home. Next, a contractor will be hired to build the house. There it is much more uncertainty in this scenario and many more potential outcomes for this project. The individual can have whatever they want.

Creativity effort is certainly required in this complex project. As an example of chaos, an owner may decide to build their own home with no plan, no approvals, no architect, no zoning checks and not much idea of what they are doing. In this scenario, there are many choices and the options may constantly change. Optimization of creativity is necessary in this project. Figure 2 below locates these projects on the "satisficing"/optimizing model.

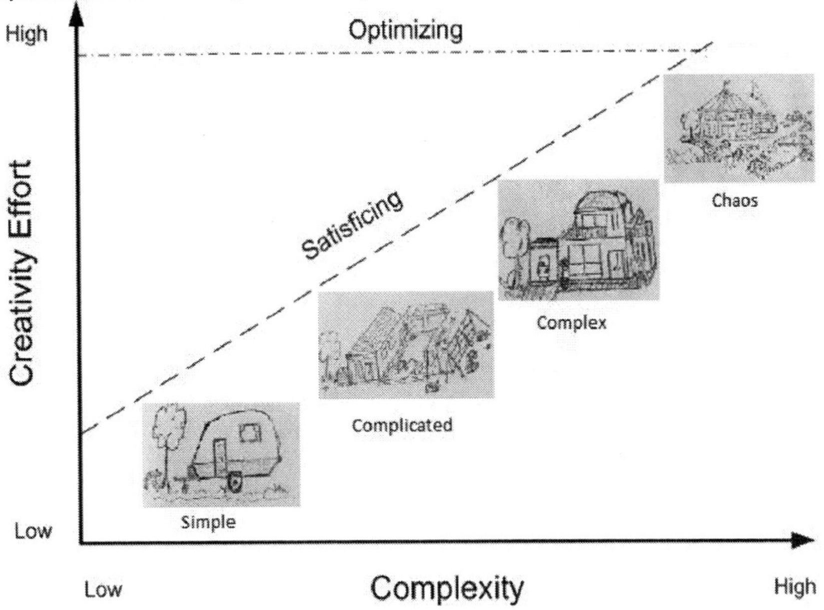

Figure 2. Examples of housing projects of differing complexity and their relationship with creativity effort

VII. CONCLUSION

This paper addresses the important issue of how much creativity is necessary under different contexts. It is commonly believed that the more creativity is generated, the better the outcome. In recent times, a high value has been placed on creative endeavors: stimulating, encouraging and financing these is seen as desirable and a measure of contribution to society. This paper presents a novel approach in suggesting that it could be more effective to map the amount of creativity effort against the nature of the project, and that not all projects require maximal stimulation of creative ideas. Based upon the complexity of the project, it will be necessary to decide how much creativity to generate, to minimize the wasted creativity effort. It is wise for practitioners and managers to assess the level of complexity in any given project, and to adjust investment in the generation of creative ideas accordingly. This can lead to a viable return on investment related to creativity effort within project management.

The practical strength of this paper is that it generates a rule which will help project managers to know how to allocate creativity efforts in line with the complexity of the project. In terms of theoretical contribution, the paper has deconstructed the idea that fostering creativity is necessarily good. The paper has demystified creativity by putting a financial value on it. The concept of parsimony is relevant here. This theory separates out the action from its value. The paper is moving away from an evaluation of creativity on its own merits towards an evaluation of creativity as an ability to solve a problem and move forward. Putting a practical and financial value on creativity challenges the current view which places creativity on a pedestal in terms of its value to society.

ACKNOWLEDGEMENT

The authors would like to thank Dr. Rosemary Hallo for the illustrations in Figure 2.

REFERENCES

[1] B. Whittaker, "What went wrong? Unsuccessful information technology projects," *Information Management & Computer Security*, vol. 7, pp. 23-30, 1999.

[2] G. Tan, "Managing Creativity in Organizations: a Total System Approach," *Creativity and Innovation Management*, vol. 7, pp. 23-31, 1998.

[3] A. H. Y. Hon, "Does job creativity requirement improve service performance? A multilevel analysis of work stress and service environment," *International Journal of Hospitality Management*, vol. 35, pp. 161-170, 2013/12/01.

[4] A. Einsiedel Jr., "Profile of effective project managers," *Project Management Journal*, vol. 18, pp. 51-56, 1987.

[5] Y. L. Wong and K. W. M. Siu, "A model of creative design process for fostering creativity of students in design education," *International Journal of Technology and Design Education*, vol. 22, pp. 437-450, 2012.

[6] L. Gabora, "Research on Creativity," in *Encyclopedia of Creativity, Invention, Innovation and Entrepreneurship*, E. G.

Carayannis, Ed., ed New York, NY: Springer New York, 2013, pp. 1548-1558.
[7] T. J. Howard, S. J. Culley, and E. Dekoninck, "Describing the creative design process by the integration of engineering design and cognitive psychology literature," *Design Studies,* vol. 29, pp. 160-180, 3/2008.
[8] T. M. Amabile and M. G. Pratt, "The dynamic componential model of creativity and innovation in organizations: Making progress, making meaning," *Research in Organizational Behavior,* vol. 36, pp. 157-183, 2016.
[9] C. Andriopoulos, "Determinants of organisational creativity: a literature review," *Management Decision,* vol. 39, pp. 834-841, 2001.
[10] E. S. Metzl and M. A. Morrell, "The Role of Creativity in Models of Resilience: Theoretical Exploration and Practical Applications," *Journal of Creativity in Mental Health,* vol. 3, pp. 303-318, 2008/10/10.
[11] M. Csikszentmihalyi, "A systems perspective on creativity," in *Handbook of creativity*, S. R, Ed., ed Cambridge: Cambridge University press, 1997, pp. 313 - 335.
[12] R. Bratvold and S. Begg, *Making good decisions*. Texas, USA: Society of petroleum engineers, 2010.
[13] H. Simon, "Rational choice and the structure of the environment," *Psychological Review,* vol. 63, 1956.
[14] H. Simon, *Administrative behaviour: a study of decision-making processes in administrative organisations*, 4th ed. New York: The Free Press, 2013.
[15] D. J. Snowden and M. E. Boone, "A Leader's Framework for Decision Making. (cover story)," *Harvard Business Review,* vol. 85, pp. 68-76, 2007.
[16] H. Volberda, "Building a flexible firm: how to remain competitive," *Corporate Reputation Review,* 1998.
[17] B. Gray, "The Cynefin framework: applying an understanding of complexity to medicine," *Journal of Primary Health Care,* vol. 9, pp. 258-261, 2017.
[18] M. Efatmaneshnik and M. Ryan, "A general framework for measuring system complexity," *Complexity,* vol. 21, pp. 533-546, 2016.
[19] D. Sachau, "Resurrecting the Motivation-Hygiene Theory: Herzberg and the Positive Psychology Movement," *Human Resource Development Review,* vol. 6, pp. 377-393, 2007/12/01.
[20] A. H. Y. Hon, "Shaping Environments Conductive to Creativity:The Role of Intrinsic Motivation," *Cornell Hospitality Quarterly,* vol. 53, pp. 53-64, 2012.
[21] M. Uhl-Bien and R. Marion, "Complexity leadership in bureaucratic forms of organizing: A meso model," *The Leadership Quarterly,* vol. 20, pp. 631-650, 2009/08/01.
[22] M. Uhl-Bien, R. Marion, and B. McKelvey, "Complexity Leadership Theory: Shifting leadership from the industrial age to the knowledge era," *The Leadership Quarterly,* vol. 18, pp. 298-318, 2007/08/01.
[23] A. Mark and D. Snowden, *Researching Practice or Practicing Research: Innovating Methods in Healthcare - The Contribution of Cynefin*, 2006.
[24] W. R. Ashby, *Variety, constraint, and the law of requisite variety.* Chicago: Aldine, 1968.
[25] W. R. Ashby, "Requisite Variety and Its Implications for the Control of Complex Systems," in *Facets of Systems Science*, ed Boston, MA: Springer US, 1991, pp. 405-417.
[26] A. Gorod, T. Nguyen, and L. Hallo, "Systems engineering decision-making: Optimizing and/or satisficing?," in *2017 Annual IEEE International Systems Conference (SysCon)*, 2017, pp. 1-6.

Using Adaptive Immersive Environments to Stimulate Emotional Expression and Connection in Dementia Care

Insights from User Perspectives towards SENSE-GARDEN

Gemma Goodall[1], Ileana Ciobanu[2], Ronny Broekx[3], Jon Sørgaard[1], Iulian Anghelache[4], Catalina Anghelache-Tutulan[4], Mara Diaconu[4], Sigrid Mæland[5], Therese Borve[5], Audun Digranes Dagestad[5], Piet Bormans[6], Marleen Custers[6], Katrin Losleben[7], Rita Valadas[8], Alda Matias[8], Andreea Marin[2], Kristin Taraldsen[1], Walter Maetzler[9], Mihai Berteanu[2], J. Artur Serrano[1,10]

[1]Department of Neuromedicine and Movement Science, Faculty of Medicine and Health, Norwegian University of Science and Technology
[2]University of Medicine and Pharmacy Carol Davila, Bucharest, ELIAS University Hospital, Romania
[3]Innovation Department, ePoint, Belgium
[4] Research & Development Department, Compexin SA, Romania
[5]Odda Municipality
[6]Aan de Beverdijk, Vulpia Vlaanderen
[7]Kvinnforsk, University Hospital of North Norway
[8]Santa Casa da Misericórdia de Lisboa
[9]Department of Neurology, Christian-Albrechts-University, Kiel, Germany
[10]Norwegian Centre for eHealth Research, University Hospital of North Norway

Email: gemma.goodall@ntnu.no, ileanacuk@yahoo.co.uk, ronny.broekx@gmail.com, jon.sorgaard@ntnu.no, a.iulian@compexin.ro, catalina.anghelache@compexin.ro, mara.manailescu@compexin.ro, sigrid.meland@odda.kommune.no, therese.borve@odda.kommune.no, audun.digranes.dagestad@odda.kommune.no, piet.bormans@beverdijk.be, marleen.custers@beverdijk.be, katrin@losleben.eu, rita.valadas@scml.pt, alda.matias@scml.pt, andreea.budrica@gmail.com, kristin.taraldsen@ntnu.no, w.maetzler@neurologie.uni-kiel.de, mberteanu@gmail.com, artur.serrano@ntnu.no

***Abstract*— This paper presents early stage research on the development of an immersive, multisensory room for people living with dementia. Dementia is considered to be a public health priority on a global level. Our research addresses the challenge of meeting individual needs in dementia care, particularly in relation to social and emotional wellbeing. We draw upon findings from 52 interviews with users, including people with mild cognitive impairment, professional caregivers, and informal caregivers. These interviews were conducted to explore initial responses towards a multisensory room called SENSE-GARDEN. Findings indicate that users view the immersive environment as a space in which a person with dementia's sense of self can be supported and expressed with others. SENSE-GARDEN was considered to be a tool for creating emotional environments in which users can explore their life stories together with loved ones. Technology's role in fostering emotional spaces is discussed in terms of a transactional relationship between the person with dementia, the caregiver, and the immersive environment. This research provides rationale for the study of emotional engagement and interaction not only in the SENSE-GARDEN project, but also in the wider context of welfare technology as a whole.**

Keywords-dementia; virtual environments; immersive technology; emotions; interpersonal relationships

I. INTRODUCTION

Dementia is an umbrella term for a variety of neurodegenerative diseases that most often affect memory, behaviour, and communicative abilities [1]. There are approximately 47 million people living with dementia worldwide [2]. With this number set to increase to 131 million by 2050, it is of the utmost importance to tackle dementia's progressive impact on the wellbeing of people living with a diagnosis.

The World Health Organization has called for action on dementia, presenting it as a public health priority at a global level [1]. This action includes a call for research to identify ways of supporting the needs of people living with dementia, their caregivers, and the needs of society in the context of costs, understanding, and awareness.

In recent years, studies have identified numerous complex needs of people with dementia living in long-term care. These include management of challenging behaviours, maintenance of social relationships, involvement of people with cognitive deficits in meaningful activities, and supporting the emotional needs of all [3][4].

Emotion-oriented approaches to care have been shown to be cost-effective ways of improving psychological wellbeing and social behaviour amongst people with dementia [5][6]. These nonpharmacological approaches are often person-centred, focusing on the social and emotional needs of the individual. Reminiscence rooms, virtual gardens and virtual reality forests are examples of how immersive technologies have been integrated in emotion-oriented approaches designed to create effective interventions for people with dementia [7][8].

However, this area of study has called for further research in determining what works best for the individual [9]. It has recently been suggested that an individualized multisensory environment for people with dementia would be a highly beneficial intervention, especially if family members are included in the selection of stimuli [10]. Our research builds on this suggestion, creating not only a personalized multisensory intervention, but one which also incorporates immersive technology, all with the inclusion of family members, friends, and professional care staff.

This paper presents early stage research on a multisensory room, SENSE-GARDEN, that is currently being developed as an adaptive, immersive environment integrating technology and multisensory stimulation for reminiscence in people living with dementia. We will first provide a brief overview of the project (Section II), followed by the description of the methodology used in research and development (Section III). We will then discuss the results of the interviews in terms of self-identity (Section IV) and shared emotional experiences (Section V). In Section VI, these results are summarised and discussed in the theoretical frame of a transactional relationship between users and the immersive environment. Finally, in Section VII, we conclude with final remarks, the next steps for SENSE-GARDEN, and suggestions for future research.

II. SENSE-GARDEN: An Overview

SENSE-GARDEN is a psychosocial intervention that is being developed to create individualized reminiscence sessions for people living with dementia in residential care. The intervention combines the use of technology for reminiscence and multisensory stimulation, with human-to-human informational and emotional communication.

Prototypes of the SENSE-GARDEN room are currently being built across Belgium, Norway, Portugal and Romania. These rooms are filled with individualized stimuli such as familiar music, imagery, films and scents in order to stimulate memory and encourage active participation of the person with dementia in reminiscing activities. Particular emphasis is placed on using autobiographical content such as family photographs, music from childhood, and films of life events.

The use of large projection screens, scent dispensers, and surround sound systems will integrate the various multimedia of the room, creating an immersive environment. For example, high-definition imagery of a forest could be accompanied with the smell of pine trees and the sound of birds.

SENSE-GARDEN will expand on currently established sensory rooms, which are also known as 'Snoezelen' rooms. Deriving from the Dutch terms for 'sniffing' and 'dozing', Snoezelen was originally developed in the Netherlands as a therapy for individuals with learning difficulties [11].

SENSE-GARDEN presents an innovative approach to sensory rooms by utilising smart technologies that enable the space to adapt to individual preferences and needs of the person with dementia. Radio frequency identification (RFID) will be used to allow the SENSE-GARDEN system to identify the user. Upon entering the room, the system will automatically project autobiographical multimedia from the person with dementia's user profile.

The room is designed to be used by two main categories of users. The first is the person with dementia (PwD), who is also considered the primary user. The second is the caregiver, who will either be informal (family/friend) or formal (professional care staff). It is anticipated that together, the PwD-caregiver dyad will interact with the immersive environment to stimulate memory, conversation, sharing and engagement.

III. Methodological Approach

SENSE-GARDEN is a multidisciplinary project involving partners in Belgium, Norway, Portugal, and Romania. The consortium brings together multiple professions and competencies including technology development, architecture, care home management, health sciences and research.

There have been numerous calls to involve people with dementia in the process of designing assistive technologies [12][13]. Their contributions are thought to be of crucial importance, along with input from their caregivers [14]. More recently, user-centred design has been recommended for the development and implementation of psychosocial interventions [15].

The SENSE-GARDEN project embraces a user-centred design and is working co-creatively with user groups throughout all its phases. The aim of this preliminary research was to explore initial responses from user groups, so that their ideas and feedback may be integrated into the development of SENSE-GARDEN.

Thus far, 52 qualitative semi-structured interviews have been conducted with user groups across Belgium, Norway, Portugal, and Romania. The aims of these interviews were to collect responses and attitudes towards the SENSE-GARDEN room concept, and to identify challenges that may arise during the course of the project.

The specific research questions for this study were as follows: (1) What are the users' attitudes towards the concept of SENSE-GARDEN? (2) What benefits, if any, do users think SENSE-GARDEN could provide in the care of people living with dementia? In order to answer these research questions, the interview was designed in a way that allowed for in-depth exploration of the users' beliefs surrounding SENSE-GARDEN. The interviews were semi-structured with open-ended questions, and lasted for approximately 30 minutes. Interview questions focused on the overall concept of SENSE-GARDEN, the individual components of the

TABLE I. RESPONDENT INFORMATION

Country	People with Mild Cognitive Impairment				Informal Caregivers				Formal Caregivers			
	N	Mean Age	Gender		N	Mean Age	Gender		N	Mean Age	Gender	
			Male	Female			Male	Female			Male	Female
Belgium	3	89.6	2	1	6	57	1	5	4	31.5	1	3
Norway	4	84	0	4	4	59.3	0	4	4	38.8	1	3
Portugal	3	79.7	0	3	3	55.7	0	3	3	44.3	0	3
Romania	6	67.2	3	3	6	50.7	0	6	6	42.7	2	4
Total	**16**	**77.9**	**5**	**11**	**19**	**55.3**	**1**	**18**	**17**	**39.4**	**4**	**13**

intervention, and potential benefits.

The respondents included 16 people living with a diagnosis of mild cognitive impairment (MCI), 19 informal caregivers, and 17 professional caregivers. In this study, informal caregivers are defined as individuals who are the spouse, relative, or close friend of a person living with dementia or MCI. Professional caregivers are individuals working within environments that administer care for people living with dementia.

Table 1 gives an overview of the respondent information. Despite the relatively small sample size, a diversity of age groups are represented. There is a visible age difference across the three user groups, with almost 20 years in between each. The majority of the respondents were women, especially within the two caregiving groups.

In order to conduct an in-depth exploration of the ideas and perspectives given by the users, data was analysed using thematic analysis. Thematic analysis is a qualitative method in which prevalent patterns of ideas and responses are identified amongst data. The analysis procedure for this study undertook the following phases, given by Braun and Clarke [16]:

1) Familiarisation with the data: All the data was thoroughly read and re-read, along with notating initial ideas and interpretations of the dataset

2) Coding: The ideas were used to generate codes, which identify interesting features across the data. In this study, data was manually coded in an inductive manner, meaning that the codes and themes were developed directly from the content of the data, rather than being developed by pre-existing ideas.

3) Searching for themes: The codes were used to search for themes, which represent patterned responses or meanings across the data.

4) Reviewing themes: The themes were reviewed to ensure that they accurately represent the views of the users and the view from the entire dataset.

5) Defining and naming themes: The essence of each theme was identified, along with its relevance to the research questions.

6) Producing the report: Finally, the themes are considered in their relationship to one another, and a narrative about the dataset is created. This narrative is supported by direct quotes from the dataset.

In order to stay true to the 'voice' of the users, codes and themes were constantly checked back against the original data. Braun and Clarke [16] emphasize the importance of the flexibility in thematic analysis and identify the process as one of continuous reflection on the reading, shaping, and checking of data and themes.

Six themes were generated from analysis: (1) benefits for all, (2) past and present, (3) focus on the individual, (4) shared experiences, (5) emotional stimulation, and (6) challenges to consider. Given its strong prevalence and common occurrence across all themes, this short paper will focus on user feedback regarding emotion. Results will be discussed in terms of recovering self-identity and expressing and sharing emotional experiences.

The full dataset from the interviews has been made available online, along with the interview guide, and coding from thematic analysis [17].

IV. RECOVERING SELF-IDENTITY

Dementia's impact on memory, behaviour and communicative abilities can have detrimental implications for a person's identity. However, there is evidence to suggest that individuals may preserve a sense of self to some extent, even in more severe stages of dementia [18][19]. In discussing the benefits of SENSE-GARDEN, all respondents believed that the individualized nature of the virtual environment could trigger autobiographical memories. This was linked by the respondents to helping people with dementia connect with their past: "Just only three notes will bring back that special moment"..., "Personal videos and photos are important. You resonate with your past."

Respondents considered interaction with the past as an activity for strengthening self-identity in the present moment: "Nowadays we forget who we are. SENSE-GARDEN will help us all relive forgotten events and identities"..., "Awareness of time passing by associating the child in the past with today the adult." This strengthening of selfhood was also considered to 'bring back' the person with dementia, as if a separate identity existed prior to the onset of the disease: "Family and friends can be with the patient as they were before".

This symbiotic relationship between past and present has been much discussed in regards to selfhood. Surr [18] adopts a socio-biographical approach to explain how people with dementia use their past in the context of telling their life story to others, in order to maintain a sense of self in the present.

Along with allowing family members to be reconnected with their loved one, there was an impression that professional caregivers would also be able to view the person with dementia in a modified perspective, after sharing life story experiences: "Good for the staff to see the person with dementia in another way". Digital storytelling, an activity in which technology is used to create innovative forms of narrative, has been shown to educate nursing home staff [20].

The role of others should not be underestimated in maintaining the identity of the person with dementia. In discussing the needs of people with dementia, Kitwood [21] stresses the importance of others in the maintenance of personhood. Westius, Kallenberg, and Norburg [22] present the notion of 'intertwined narrative', in which the life story of the person with dementia is integrated with the narrative of their family carer. Thus, if the person with dementia should become unable to independently recall their story, the intertwined narrative of the caring relationship may provide opportunity for maintenance of self.

Earlier literature presents similar ideas. Mills [23] suggests that people with dementia bestow their life stories to another, therefore continuing their sense of identity. Mills states that in this sense, the narrative of the individual never disappears, regardless of the inevitable fading of the person's memory.

SENSE-GARDEN could potentially offer a method for assisting family and friends in preserving the life story of the person with dementia. Additionally, SENSE-GARDEN offers the opportunity for individuals to explore their life story in a new and innovative way (through the use of interactive touchscreens, immersive film and sound): "We can explore old and new places"..., "My mother wants to see her old street again but we can't do it, with this she can visit it again"

V. Expressing and Sharing Emotional Experiences

The users' value for sharing experiences together resonated across all of the interviews. Respondents saw SENSE-GARDEN as a means to alleviating communicative issues in the caring relationship: "It's hard being a relative, so little competence, dialogue is difficult. This is a great tool for having a nice time together"..., "If I visit, there are always dead moments. This will help get the life back into the conversations". SENSE-GARDEN's perceived ability to revive communication suggests technology may act as a catalyst for emotional connection. This was echoed in other responses regarding relationships: "It improves relationships with others"..., "Sharing the experience is the most important for reconnecting".

SENSE-GARDEN was also considered as a potentially helpful tool for stimulating nonverbal communication and expression. There was a particular emphasis on the ability to express oneself through the use of imagery and music: "Being able to tell stories, if one has lost the language, pictures and movies can tell things"..., "Some people stop talking, but they can sing."

Individuals living with the disease are capable of experiencing and expressing a wide range of emotions, even in later stages of dementia [5][24]. Incorporating creative activity into the immersive environment has the potential to elicit positive expressions of emotion and of self.

However, one respondent with mild cognitive impairment brought an important consideration to light in stating that the facilitation from the caregiver is vital for the success of the intervention: "The therapist is very important and can instil peace and wellbeing. A special emotional environment must be created for SENSE-GARDEN to work." This concept of creating a 'special emotional environment' goes to suggest that it is not the intervention alone that can benefit the caring relationship, but also the individuals present who can shape the experience of SENSE-GARDEN.

This idea is supported by respondents' concepts of 'space' as something more than just a physical environment: "SENSE-GARDEN is an intermediary space, between memories and the here and now, a space we can all access and we can remember how to feel, by one's self and together, without shame or fear."

The above quote, given by an informal caregiver, encapsulates the essence of what SENSE-GARDEN is aiming to achieve. By adopting a holistic approach to the environment, the individuals within it, and the relationships that take place, the project aims to create an intervention that can facilitate connection and wellbeing for all users.

VI. Discussion

These findings highlight users' values for emotional and social benefits in SENSE-GARDEN. There was an overall sense of the immersive environment being able to stimulate autobiographical memory, which was valued as important for preserving a sense of identity. The perspectives of respondents are in agreement with previous research on virtual environments for people with dementia. Siraraya and Ang [25] describe the virtual world as a 'memory sanctuary', in which selfhood and relationships are maintained.

The respondents were persistent in their beliefs that the environment, the facilitation of the intervention, and the stimuli all need to be tailored to the specific traits of the person with dementia visiting the SENSE-GARDEN. It should be acknowledged that the task of individualization is not an easy feat. As human beings, we are all individualistic by nature, with different tastes, preferences, and desires. Adding the constantly fluctuating progression of dementia to this individuality makes for a difficult task in designing technology for these users [26][27]. This is something that the SENSE-GARDEN project will have to tackle through rigorous work and collaboration with users, technology developers, and researchers of various disciplines.

Respondents also emphasized the importance of interaction between the SENSE-GARDEN stimuli, the person with dementia, and the caregiver. The way in which an environment simultaneously influences behaviour of individuals and interpersonal relationships, and yet is shaped by those persons, can be referred to as the transactional relationship.

The notion of 'transaction' was firstly used in this context by the philosopher John Dewey, who asserted "Everything that exists in far as it is known and knowable is in interaction with other things. It is associated, as well as solitary, single." [28]. In the context of SENSE-GARDEN, it could be said that a transactional relationship exists between the various technologies (the immersive environment), the person with dementia, and the caregiver.

This transactional relationship is conceptualized visually in Figure 1. The figure shows how numerous interactions may take place between each user and SENSE-GARDEN to form an overall relationship. The SENSE-GARDEN system is influenced by the users, but, at the same time, the users' emotions and interpersonal interaction with each other are shaped by the immersive environment that SENSE-GARDEN creates.

Later literature on emotion echoes Dewey's view, suggesting a need to study the complex relationship between person and environment, for emotions cannot be comprehended by one or the other alone [29]. These ideas can be linked to current thought on the nature of technology design, which has been described as 'deeply contextual' [27]. Therefore, incorporating the study of context, environment and relationships seems appropriate for both dementia studies and technology development.

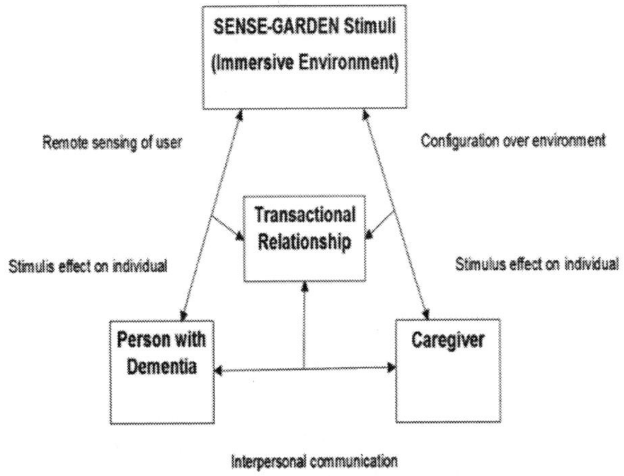

Figure 1. Conceptual model of the transactional relationship that takes place within the SENSE-GARDEN intervention

Understanding the interaction between environment and the people within it is vital. How does SENSE-GARDEN, and technology as a whole, fit into this interaction? What role does it play? Going forward, research should adopt a holistic approach to evaluating technology, considering the wider context in which the technology is situated.

VII. Conclusion and Future Work

The user interviews yielded valuable insights for the progression of the SENSE-GARDEN project, with findings demonstrating the importance that users hold for emotional and social wellbeing. This paper has demonstrated the value and usefulness of including user groups in the development of not only immersive spaces, but also of interventions for care.

Finally, the social and emotional aspects of virtual environments should not be underestimated. The results highlight the significance users find in fostering relationships through means of self-identity and emotional relationships. A focus on social and emotional interactions between technology, users, and interpersonal relationships could provide very fruitful results in the context of dementia care. This research provides rationale for the study of emotional engagement and interaction not only in the SENSE-GARDEN project, but also in the wider context of welfare technology studies.

Acknowledgment

This study was performed in the frame of the EU project SENSE-GARDEN (AAL/Call2016/054-b/2017, with implementation period June 2017 - May 2020) funded by AAL Programme, co-funded by the European Commission and National Funding Authorities of Norway, Belgium, Romania, and Portugal.

We would like to thank all participants in the study.

References

[1] World Health Organization, "Global action plan on the public health response to dementia 2017-2025." Geneva: World Health Organization, 2017.

[2] M. Prince, "World Alzheimer Report 2015: the global impact of dementia: an analysis of prevalence, incidence, costs and trends.", Alzheimer's Disease International, 2015.

[3] M. Cadieux, L. Garcia, and J. Patrick, "Needs of People With Dementia in Long-Term Care", American Journal of Alzheimer's Disease & Other Dementias, vol. 28, no. 8, pp. 723-733, Sep. 2013, doi: 10.1177/1533317513500840

[4] R. Milte et al., "Quality in residential care from the perspective of people living with dementia: The importance of personhood", Archives of Gerontology and Geriatrics, vol. 63, pp. 9-17, Mar-Apr, 2016.

[5] K. Lee, D. Algase, and E. McConnell, "Daytime Observed Emotional Expressions of People With Dementia", Nursing Research, vol. 62, no. 4, pp. 218-225, Jul-Aug. 2013, doi: 10.1097/NNR.0b013e31829999d7

[6] E. Finnema, R. Dröes, M. Ribbe, and W. Van Tilburg, "The effects of emotion-oriented approaches in the care for persons

suffering from dementia: a review of the literature", International Journal of Geriatric Psychiatry, vol. 15, no. 2, pp. 141-161, 2000.

[7] G. Gowans et al., "Designing a multimedia conversation aid for reminiscence therapy in dementia care environments" in CHI '04 Extended Abstracts on Human Factors in Computing Systems (CHI EA '04), ACM, April. 2004, pp. 825-836, ISBN: 1-58113-703-6.

[8] W. Moyle, C. Jones, T. Dwan, and T. Petrovich, "Effectiveness of a Virtual Reality Forest on People With Dementia: A Mixed Methods Pilot Study", The Gerontologist, vol. 00, no. 00, pp. 1-10, Mar. 2017, doi: 10.1093/geront/gnw270

[9] D. Smit, J. de Lange, B. Willemse, J. Twisk, and A. Pot, "Activity involvement and quality of life of people at different stages of dementia in long term care facilities", Aging & Mental Health, vol. 20, no. 1, pp. 100-109, Jun. 2015, doi: 10.1080/13607863.2015.1049116

[10] Y. Cui, M. Shen, Y. Ma, and S. Wen, "Senses make sense: An individualized multisensory stimulation for dementia", Medical Hypotheses, vol. 98, pp. 11-14, Jan. 2017.

[11] J. Hulsegge and A. Verheul, "Snoezelen: Another World", Chestefield, UK: Rompa, 2005

[12] R. Orpwood, "Involving People with Dementia in the Design Process- Examples of Iterative Design", in Dementia, Design and Technology, P. Topo and B. Östlund, Ed. IOS Press, 2009, pp. 79-95.

[13] M. Span, M. Hettinga, M. Vernooij-Dassen, J. Eefsting, and C. Smits, "Involving people with dementia in the development of supportive IT applications: A systematic review", Ageing Research Reviews, vol. 12, no. 2, pp. 535-551, Mar. 2013, doi: 10.1016/j.arr.2013.01.002

[14] M. Marshall, "The Needs of People with Dementia and Their Carers and the Potential Role of Design and Technology", in Dementia, Design and Technology, P. Topo and B. Östlund, Ed. IOS Press, 2009, pp. 3-8.

[15] A. Lyon and K. Koerner, "User-Centered Design for Psychosocial Intervention Development and Implementation", Clinical Psychology: Science and Practice, vol. 23, no. 2, pp. 180-200, Jun. 2016, doi: 10.1111/cpsp.12154

[16] V. Braun and V. Clarke, "Using thematic analysis in psychology", Qualitative Research in Psychology, vol. 3, no. 2, pp. 77-101, 2006.

[17] G. Goodall et al., "Dataset for "Using Adaptive Immersive Environments to Stimulate Emotional Expression and Connection in Dementia Care: Insights from User Perspectives towards SENSE-GARDEN" [Data set]. Zenodo. doi:10.5281/zenodo.1232156

[18] C. Surr, "Preservation of self in people with dementia living in residential care: A socio-biographical approach", Social Science & Medicine, vol. 62, no. 7, pp. 1720-1730, 2006

[19] L. Caddell and L. Clare, "The impact of dementia on self and identity: A systematic review", Clinical Psychology Review, vol. 30, no. 1, pp. 113-126, Feb. 2010.

[20] R. Stenhouse, J. Tait, P. Hardy, and T. Sumner, "Dangling conversations: reflections on the process of creating digital stories during a workshop with people with early-stage dementia", Journal of Psychiatric and Mental Health Nursing, vol. 20, no. 2, pp. 134-141, Mar. 2012, doi: 10.1111/j.1365-2850.2012.01900.x

[21] T. Kitwood, "The experience of dementia", Aging & Mental Health, vol. 1, no. 1, pp. 13-22, 1997.

[22] A. Westius, K. Kallenberg, and A. Norberg, "Views of life and sense of identity in people with Alzheimer's disease", Ageing and Society, vol. 30, no. 07, pp. 1257-1278, Jul. 2010, doi: 10.1017/S0144686X10000309

[23] M. Mills, "Narrative Identity and Dementia: a Study of Emotion and Narrative in Older People with Dementia", Ageing and Society, vol. 17, no. 6, pp. 673-698, Nov. 1997.

[24] R. Woods, "Discovering the person with Alzheimer's disease: Cognitive, emotional and behavioural aspects", Aging & Mental Health, vol. 5, no. 1, pp. 7-16, 2001.

[25] P. Siriaraya and C. S. Ang, "Recreating living experiences from past memories through virtual worlds for people with dementia", in Proceedings of the SIGCHI Conference on Human Factors in Computing Systems, ACM, April 2014, pp. 3977-3986

[26] L. Nygård, "Living with Dementia and the Challenges of Domestic Technology", in Dementia, Design and Technology, P. Topo and B. Östlund, Ed. IOS Press, 2009, pp. 9-25

[27] T. Jiancaro, S. Jaglal, and A. Mihailidis, "Technology, design and dementia: an exploratory survey of developers", Disability and Rehabilitation: Assistive Technology, vol. 12, no. 6, pp. 573-584, Jun. 2016, doi: 10.1080/17483107.2016.1187671

[28] J. Dewey, Experience and Nature. Courier Corporation, 1958.

[29] R. Lazarus and S. Folkman, "Transactional theory and research on emotions and coping", European Journal of Personality, vol. 1, no. 3, pp. 141-169, Sep. 1987, doi: 10.1002/per.2410010304

Mobile Technology to Support Didactic Strategies

Bianca Carvalho Martins
Geane Santana Rocha Quixabeira
Leysson Muriel Tavares Guimarães Barros
Claudio de Castro Monteiro
Federal Institute of Education, Science and Technology of Tocantins (IFTO) Palmas
IT department
Palmas, Brazil
e-mail: {bianca.etf, geanezinha, leyssonm}@gmail.com
e-mail: ccm@ifto.edu.br

Abstract — **This paper discusses the uses of the results of external assessments in educational assignments to improve the quality of elementary teaching. The challenge of disseminating such results is highlighted in an intuitive and attractive way. It also refers to the repercussions of the implemented mobile application, which is aimed at improving the current educational environment. In this way, the importance of the use of technologies in numerous areas, in this case, in education, is proven with the development of this work. The elaborate mobile application was tested and evaluated by the target audience of interest and the article shows the results obtained through the evaluation.**

Keywords-application; external assessments; educational quality.

I. INTRODUCTION

Education evaluation in Brazil has become a State policy based on the reforms, policies and educational actions implemented since the 1990s. Since then, discussions about Brazilian educational problems in both basic education and higher education have been based on the dissemination of information produced by the evaluation processes implemented, with a focus on large-scale, centralized and standardized exams, pointing out the students' strengths, profit and are expressed by rates in scores form or concepts.

It has been emphasized that from the 1970s the post-graduate *stricto sensu* had already had an assessment led by the Coordination of Improvement of Higher Level Personnel (Capes). Basic education began to be evaluated by the Basic Education Assessment System (Saeb) and the higher by the National System for the Assessment of Higher Education (Sinaes).

After this process, everyone became involved in the planning of didactic situations that favor development of the competences and skills that have not yet been built or that are in the process of construction. Therefore, this allows the teacher to carry out real and significant interventions through diversified tasks, bringing about critical and collective reflection for overcoming difficulties and for advancing towards improvement in learning.

Education and technology came to be seen no longer separately, but as a necessary alliance. Teaching practice has changed constantly as new demands and learning needs as well as great amounts of information acquired at a surprising speed. Thinking about it, the teacher, who needs to master these changes and has little time, also needs the support of technology to optimize time, find interesting content, prepare lessons, communicate with students and more. The tool created to help access the information of the evaluations already mentioned thus helps to inform the daily planning of the teacher for the classroom.

This paper has the objective of examining the assessment system for basic education in Brazil, with emphasis on the Palmas Educational Assessment System-SAEP. Besides presenting concepts and objectives of the main systems of assessment, it tries to discuss some of weaknesses in the way that the data are made available. The paper was divided into the following forms: In Section 2, the assignments are related. In Section 3, the proposal is presented for creating of the tool. I Section 4, the methodology used for creation and implementation of the tool are shown. Section 5 presents the results through the use of its didactic application, closing in Sections 6 and 7 with the acknowledgment, future assignments and references.

II. RELATED ASSIGNMENTS

The Saeb introduced in the early 1990s was initially based on the quantitative results of a test applied to a sample of students and was changed in 2005. There were two components: the National Assessment of Basic Education (Aneb). This is a large-scale examination applied in a sample of schools, and the National Assessment of School Income (Anresc), known as the Brazil Test, which is also a large-scale examination applied to all students. The Brazil Test was introduced in 2005 as an evaluation instrument based on the application of large-scale exams in order to evaluate the performance in Portuguese and Mathematics of all students enrolled in the educational systems, which made it possible to disseminate the results by school unit. In 2007, the Basic Education Development Index (Ideb) was introduced, which began to combine the results of the students in the examinations of the Brazil Test with the approval rates by school (school flow). Based on these indicators, schools and education networks were classified on a numerical scale. Based on these two indicators - Brazil Test and school flow - the Ideb began a major media campaign, in which the instrument that indicates the quality of Brazilian basic education, also serves to mount rankings of schools and states of the federation. The policy of rankings in basic education was then established.

It is possible to develop a system of evaluation aimed at improving the quality of education - including teaching, learning and institutional management with the aim of transforming the current school into an institution dedicated and committed to the democratization of knowledge and education, as well as with the transformation of society [1]. In this way, to evaluate implies in taking of decision with a view to refining the improvement of institutional quality and providing accountability accounts the society.

In this context, contemporary theorists such as [2]-[5] have innovated conceptions of evaluation and contributed to the evolution of the teaching and learning process. In this perspective, assessment is a qualitative appreciation of relevant data in the process of teaching and learning that assists the teachers in making decisions about their work. Therefore evaluation is a reflection on the level of quality of school work. Thus, large-scale evaluation must also be perceived in the same way.

The evaluative act is thus perceived as inherent and indispensable, during any educational process that takes place in a constant work of action-reflection-action, as in [6], to educate is to act as subject, is to question the world in which we live in order overcome the contradictions, committing ourselves to this world to constantly recreate it.

Based on the history of educational assessments and the need for growth and increasing information in educational networks, the idea came about of creating a tool that facilitates the access and dissemination of important data about the evaluation system of the municipal network of Palmas -TO.

Palmas Educational Assessment System (SAEP) is characterized as an external evaluation that aims to provide consistent, periodic and comparable indicators of the Municipal Teaching Network of Palmas that can guide the agents involved in the educational system in the quest for improving the quality of teaching.

The assessment was an action requested by the Municipal Department of Education to for the Evaluation, Statistics and Training Board, aiming to present the index of non-literate students in the classes of 5th to the 9th grade of elementary school. The process was initiated based on a pre-diagnosis carried out by the teaching units of the aforementioned network, raising the abilities of students with difficulties in the construction of reading, interpretation and writing development.

The diagnostic assessment is an inquiry instrument and it intends to contribute to the construction and resignification of a differentiated understanding for the teaching and learning process and to the evaluation practice from an action-reflection-action perspective. In this regard, the diagnostic assessment is considered to be a diagnostic tool that will allow the teacher to observe and become familiar with the characteristics of the students' thinking, what they know and what they need to know in order to learn, in order to develop a diversified work and to make progress learning.

In other words, the goal is to know the real development zone (what the student has already learned and performs with independence and understanding alone). That will enable interventions in the proximal development zone (which is still in the process of maturation) and take the pupils to the potential development zone (in which the student is able to perform independently after mediated learning).

Any process that was planned in such a way makes it possible to diagnose the learner's level of learning about their writing and reading construction process. The instrument was composed of questions that assesses the student's competence and their ability to read and interpret a text, using as a mechanism the ability to find explicit information and infer implicit information. To verify the level of writing construction, the mechanism used was the ability to write canonical and non-canonical words and the production of a text.

After the application assessment instrument was carried out by the schools in question, the Board of Statistical Evaluation and Training, through specialists in the areas of Portuguese Language and Literacy carried out the correction of the task, analyzing the construction and interpretation of the student, verifying the level of each student, and then tabulating and to condensing the data.

III. PROPOSAL

Two decades ago, large-scale educational evaluations were carried out in Brazil to inform education departments in the formulation of educational policies and schools in improving pedagogical practices and management. However, it is difficult for managers and education professionals to understand the results of these assessments and to use them to subsidize educational action.

Aiming to broaden the debate and the use of evaluations as a strategy for improving quality in education, the proposal of the application aims directly at teachers offering inputs for reading the results of external evaluations and stimulating proposals that focus on improvement of educational processes.

The pedagogical reading and interpretation of external evaluation results is a starting point. Identifying, for example, the information in the Brazil Test bulletins that provide clarification about student learning broadens the perception of teaching practices, as well as management practices. This reading goes beyond knowing the averages of performance and comparing them with those of other schools and systems. This reading should direct efforts towards understanding what actually happened to that generation of students who took the test and what could have produced the result in question. This movement is what turns a result into a point of support to understand, criticize and eventually change the pedagogical process. The detailed analysis of the distribution and variability of the students' performance in the proficiency scales is what makes the difference in reading and interpreting the results, and what enables a deeper knowledge of the school performance and from this, to make decisions and rethink interventions.

Little is known about the consequences and effects of evaluation policy on the organization of school work, and in particular on pedagogical action. However, some studies indicate that it is possible to affirm the existence of movements that intensify the use of external evaluations and their results by educational networks and schools in Brazil, in the articulation and organization of pedagogical work [7]-[9].

Since the release of the results of the first assessments in 1995, the researchers have had to face the challenge of disseminating them so that they could be understood by the school community, parents and all interested in knowing the levels of performance of a given population of pupils [10].

Currently, the test is being conducted and the results are passed on to the Assessment Board, which tabulates, and condenses the data and produces reports that are made available to the teacher on the site of the SAEP, where they can be worked on in the classroom. This is shown in Figure 1, below:

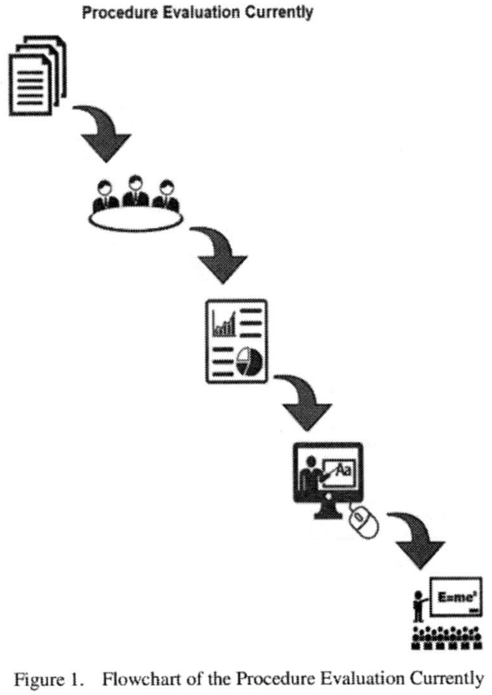

Figure 1. Flowchart of the Procedure Evaluation Currently

With the application, the test results are then passed on to a server, which interprets and presents the data on a smartphone application, more clearly and efficiently, and accessible to all teachers. This process is illustrated in Figure 2 below.

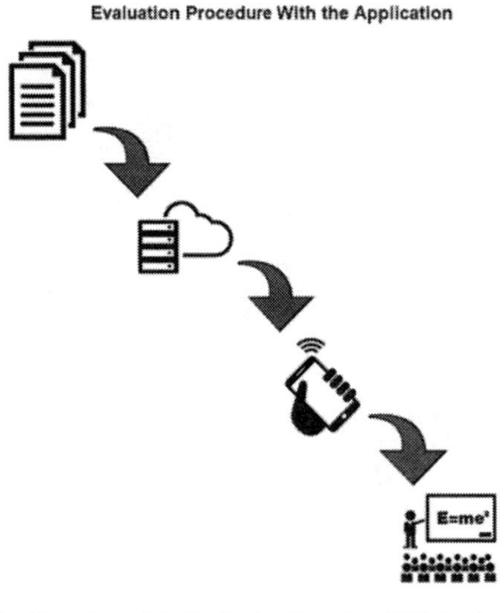

Figure 2. Flowchart of the Evaluation Procedure With the Application

Thus, the proposal of this paper is to enable the Generation of Reports on the Indicators of Quality of the Education of the System of Educational Evaluation of Palmas - SAEP, a form to facilitate the access to the information by the teacher in the classroom, making the diagnosis of the learner's level of learning more intuitive, quick and effective.

IV. METHODOLOGY

In this section, the necessary methodology will be shown on how to carry through the proposal presented in previous section 3, with the intention of later presenting the obtained results of entire process.

A. *Materials*

The materials used in this study are the following related ones:

- Computer - System Linux Ubuntu
- Ionic Framework 2.0
- JavaScript Object Notation (JSON)
- Google Forms

B. *Methods*

In this context, the Ionic is inserted in a framework for developing applications for mobile devices that aims for the implementation of hybrid applications for fast and easy development. The framework is the easiest way for the web developer to create, develop and scale multiplatform mobile applications. It offers to many libraries a simplified development and helps to produce apps with a presentable appearance, without giving much work to the developer, and does not require much knowledge, merely Hypertext Markup Language (HTML), Cascading Style Sheets (CSS) and Javascript.

The diverse advantages of if using the Ionic framework have brought about the necessity for a light format combined with its work for data exchange and makes reading simpler.

With this the applications program was developed in the Ionic framework with information consumed by a JSON archive, a light format for data exchange. JSON is in text format and is a completely independent language because it uses conventions that are familiar to C and familiar languages, including C ++, C #, Java, JavaScript, Perl, Python and many others. These properties make JSON an ideal data exchange format.

C. *Field Work*

Field research is the type of research that seeks to find information directly from the population surveyed. It is used to establish or confirm facts, reaffirm the results of previous work, solve new or existing problems, support theorems and develop new theories.

Similar to a thermometer, which shows the temperature on a scale, the Palmas Educational Assessment System is an instrument that will point out the pupil learning on a scale, more specifically, the percentage reached in the evaluated descriptors. Combining these results with the easiness of using applications, the tool was developed and then evaluated through a form.

All the Portuguese and mathematics teachers from the two schools that were presented the applications responded to the form and two others from the group of the Post-graduate *Lato Sensu* in *Telemática* of IFTO. This is shown in Figure 3.

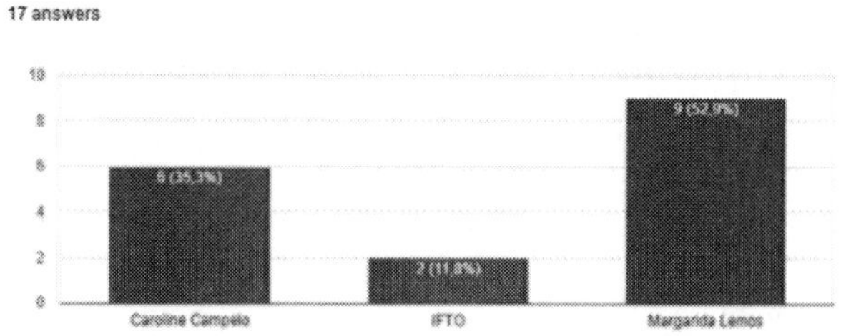

Figure 3. Amount of people per school

The form presented to the users (teachers) was answered accordingly to their opinion of the application, on a linear scale, organized accordingly to the Likert scale, ranging from 1 if they completely disagreed with the affirmation, and up to 5, in the case of full agreement.

All statements written for this research are listed below.

1. The application information is presented in a clear way.
2. The application information is of great relevance to the teacher's planning.
3. The data shown in the application makes it possible to identify where the biggest learning deficit lies in relation to the descriptor in the disciplines evaluated.
4. The navigation in the application is in an intuitive form.
5. One can always access information that is of one's own interest.
6. The application enables faster identification of the deficits of each class and consequently the implementation of possible solutions.
7. It is imagined that most people would learn to use this system quickly.
8. The students benefit from the idea of the application, where they will be able to improve in the areas of learning in which they have difficulties.
9. The information accessed will significantly contribute to quality planning in order to obtain better results in internal and external assessments.
10. Compared to the previous form of access to results, the application speeds up this access and offers a faster and more efficient way of showing and then planning for recovering or maintaining the results.

Such research had a previously calculated sample of 15 people, which counted on all teachers mentioned of the two schools presented in the application. Besides the 15 teachers, as already mentioned, two more users also answered the form.

In many cases, it is possible to determine the minimum sample size in order to estimate a statistical parameter. These formulas work with the idea that the population where the sample is located is so large that it can be considered infinite. However, many populations are not considered large enough compared to the samples, which is the case of the study in question [11]. For the circumstances already highlighted, the population available for the two schools present in the application are 15 teachers.

Thus, the formula used in this situation to determine the sample (n) was based on the average population and is shown in (1) that follows [11].

$$n = \frac{N.\sigma^2.\left(Z\frac{\alpha}{2}\right)^2}{(N-1).E^2+\sigma^2.\left(Z\frac{\alpha}{2}\right)^2} \quad (1)$$

Where:

n = Number of individuals in the sample;

N = Size of the population;

$Z\frac{\alpha}{2}$= Critical value that corresponds to the desired degree of confidence;

σ = Standard deviation of the studied variable;

E = Margin of error.

The values of all variables mentioned above are described in Table 1 below.

TABLE I. VARIABLES AND VALUES FOR THE DETERMINATION OF THE SAMPLE

Variables	Values
N	15 teachers
$Z_{\frac{\alpha}{2}}$	1,96
σ	1,18
E	0,03 (3%)
n	14,96

The critical value considered is associated with a degree of confidence of 95%. The standard deviation was determined through an assumption of the 15 teachers' answers to one of the questionings of the applied form. Thus, it reached a sample value close to 15 and which could be summed up to this value.

V. RESULTS

In this section, we will present the results, which were obtained through the application of the form described in the previous section.

The 10 statements written for the form can be related to the navigability/layout or the idea of the application, where the division was of 5 topics for each relation.

In the first evaluated scenario, the statements covered the way in which the application was presented, more precisely, its navigability and appearance. The topics that describe this situation are 1, 3, 4, 5, and 7. All the answers to the 5 affirmations of this first scenario were compiled in the graph of Figure 4 below.

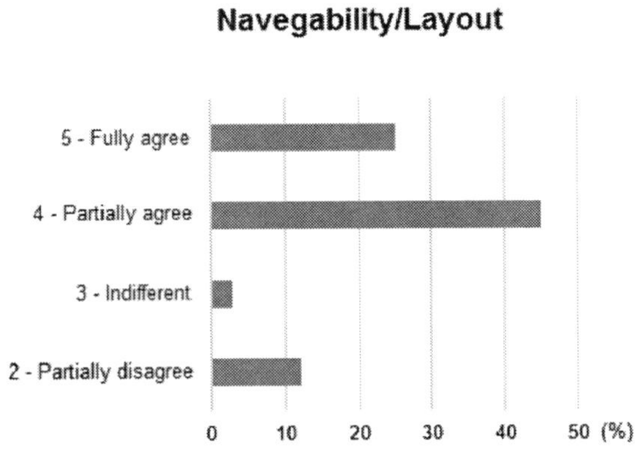

Figure 4. Results of statements related to navigability and layout

Analyzing Figure 4, it is possible to affirm that the questions obtained a considerable negative percentage. Affirmative answers were approximately 25 %, while the other 75 % had some parameters that they disagreed with. Clarity of information and access were the items that stood out most in the research as the least well evaluated. It is believed that the improvement of these two factors is essential for the application to be somewhat attractive and well spread.

In the second evaluated scenario, the idea of the application, its relevance and contribution were the items evaluated. The statements that are part of this second situation are 2, 6, 8, 9 and 10. The answers to these five affirmations can be seen in the compilation of Figure 5 that follows.

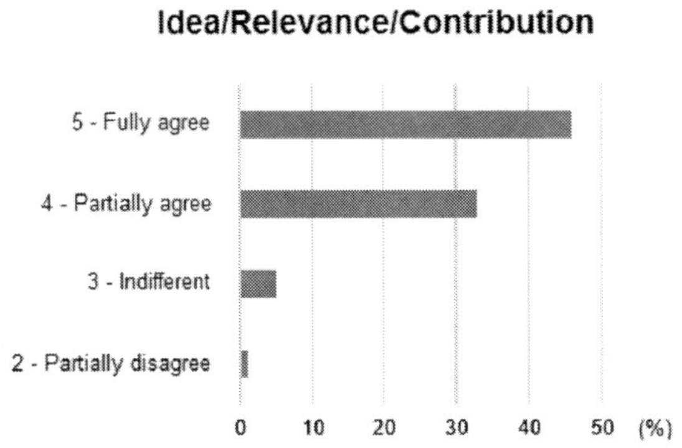

Figure 5. Results for statements related to the idea, relevance and contribution of the application

In this scenario, it is possible to realize the difference of acceptability for the situation analyzed previously. The relevance of the application is evident in the results obtained from field research. A better planning by the teacher for implementing later on a possible solution for one given situation was the most accepted item in the research.

The most rejected statement, the one with the most negative responses, is directly related to the clarity of the information in the application. The most viable explanation for such rejection is given in the little information of what the descriptors would be and what they are related to. The results are exposed directly, without a previous detailing of each line evaluated. Figure 6 shows this disagreement.

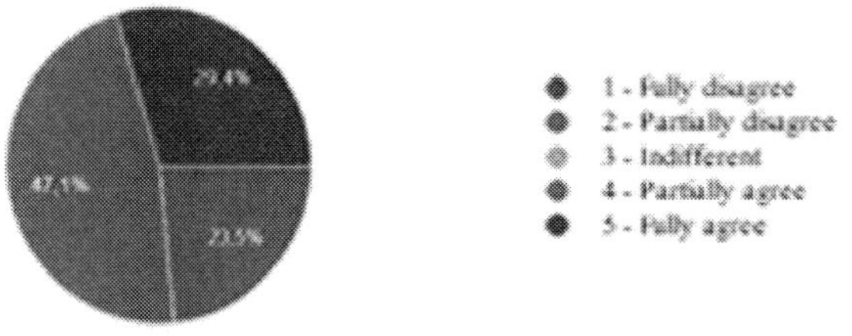

Figure 6. Result for statement 1

The most approved affirmation, and that can be considered as one of the most important, is the comparison with previous form of accessing the results. This assertion can be proved in the Figure 7.

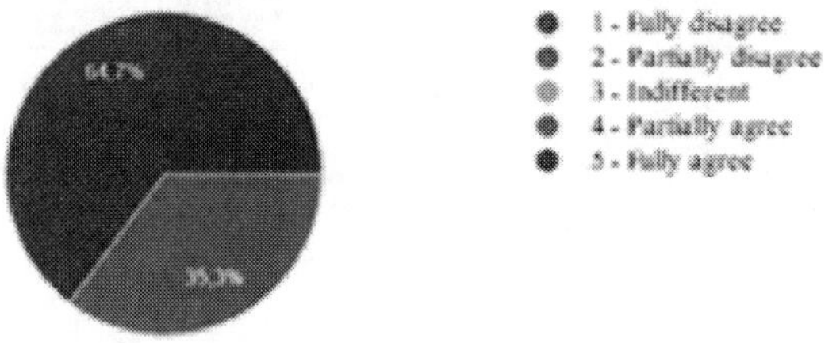

Figure 7. Result for statement 10

The test application speeds up the access to results, offers a faster and more effective way to show present and then plan to recover or keep the indicators.

VI. CONCLUSIONS

The conception of evaluation as a broad process of informing decision-making in the context of the teaching systems is recent in Brazil. It should be understood as a process that aims at contemplating skills and abilities, the curriculum itself, students study habits and the teaching strategies of the teachers. In also involves management styles of the directors and the resources they offer, to improve the performance of their work.

Evaluation is then a necessary process and condition for qualitative and quantitative targets to be established and monitored, and to ensure that the latter are reached. With this in mind, evaluation can foster in schools and networks a systematic interpellation into the quality of their practices and results, link the contributions of the external evaluation with the culture and the devices of self-evaluation of schools and strengthen their capacity to develop their autonomy, regulating the functioning of the educational system.

Thus, it is necessary to observe the information coming from the assessment as evidence of the teaching and learning process, showing the trajectories of students, schools and the network itself, in order to support pedagogical decisions and reconfigurations.

This whole scenario of strategies for the improvement of learning is facilitated by the use of technologies, making it faster to identify the deficiencies of each class in each discipline of each school. Applications such as these bring more intuitive, quick, and effective ways of identifying some problem. It is worth highlighting, therefore, the importance of investing, technologically speaking, in education in general.

Future missions will be for improving the application, both in layout and in new functions. An additional suggestion of new work is faster notifications for each specific type of user.

REFERENCES

[1] B. Isaura, M. Heitor and C. S. Luzia, "Evaluation Methodology in public policies: an experience in professional education", 3th ed. São Paulo: Cortez Publishing company, 2003.

[2] D. Lea, "The challenge of Learning Assessment: foundations for an innovative proposal", São Paulo: EPU, 1989.

[3] G. Moacir, "History of pedagogical ideas", São Paulo: Ática, 1984.

[4] H. Charles, "Demystified Evaluation", Porto Alegre: Artmed Publishing company, 2001.

[5] H. Jussara, "Evaluate to promote: the arrows of the path", Porto Alegre: Mediation, 2001.

[6] C. L. Cipriano, "Evaluation of school learning: studies and propositions", 6th Edition, São Paulo, SP: Cortez Publishing company, 1997.

[7] P. Claudia, "External evaluations and the work of pedagogical coordinators: study in a municipal network in São Paulo", 2012. Dissertation (Master in Education) - Faculty of Education, University of São Paulo, São Paulo, 2012.

[8] S. Maria, "Educational regulation: the use of proficiency results of Proeb assessments by school principals in Minas Gerais", 2011. Thesis (Doctorate in Education) - Faculty of Education, Federal University of Minas Gerais, Belo Horizonte, 2011.

[9] E. Rosimar, "There, on the table: the data of the large-scale evaluations and the mediation of the pedagogical coordinator", In: W. Flávia, "Large scale evaluation: focus on school", São Leopoldo: Oikos; Brasília: Book Liber, 2010, p. 134-146.

[10] S. F. Nilma, "The Disclosure of School System Assessment Results: Limitations and Perspectives", pp. 8, April 2013.

[11] D. M. Levine, M. L. Bereson and D. Stephan, "Statistics: Theory and Applications using Microsoft Excel in Portuguese", Rio de Janeiro: LTC, 2000.

Human Systems-of-Systems, a Methodology and Measurement Framework for Community Resilience

Tom McDermott
Stevens Institute of Technology, Systems Engineering Research Center
Hoboken, New Jersey, USA
Email: tamcdermott42@gmail.com

Abstract— **Community resilience, which focuses in on combined social and technical measures of resilience, continues to receive a great deal of attention in literature. A large number of frameworks have been developed that attempt to combine physical measures of place with measures reflecting social interaction as the basis for predictive measurement of the resilience of a community, including one from the authors. These frameworks form the basis for development of human analytics, particularly to help understand community resilience in the mitigation and preparation phases prior to disruptive events. However, very few examples of actual measurement programs are in place, and even fewer that use dynamic measures of human and social resilience. This paper builds on a methodology for characterizing human communities as Systems-of-Systems (SoS), and proposes the development of active community resilience analytics that track the continuing resilience of a community. This is a multi-scale problem, and the SoS framework is critical to development of a measurement architecture that reflects both long-term and short-term human resilience measures.**

Keywords-community resilience; resilience measurement; human analytics; systems-of-systems; sociotechnical systems.

I. INTRODUCTION

This work investigates human social analytics from a Systems-of-Systems (SoS) viewpoint using the context of community resilience. A SoS is a set of systems that interact together to produce outcomes no single system can accomplish on their own. Examples are electrical grids, rail networks, networked sensors, etc. In the resilience context, the combined community social systems, the built environment, and infrastructure systems create a large complex SoS.

Key defining features of SoS are the independence of each constituent system and the emergence of new outcomes that are unique to the whole of the SoS and not present in any individual constituent system. SoS Engineering is a discipline and methodology that seeks to define and optimize networks of interacting systems (old and new) toward common purpose and requirements [1].

This paper discusses methods and tools for "Human SoS," which addresses the interaction between networks of human and engineered systems. Understanding and classifying both the social and technical aspects of large complex systems forms the starting point for analyses of any SoS behavior. The focus on Human SoS suggests a human-centered or participatory approach to understanding and designing SoS evolutions. Human SoS methods combine aspects of Complex Systems Engineering (CSE), SoS Engineering (SoSE), and traditional Systems Engineering (SE). These present series of methods to structure and manage a set of interacting constituent systems toward a specific set of goals or purposes [2][3]. Modeling the specifically human interactions is a key to successful SoS development, but is often ignored or oversimplified in SoS design, which is why an explicit focus on Human SoS is useful.

The interaction between human community development and city infrastructure renewal in urban communities is an example context. An urban community is a shared human and engineered architecture comprised of a complex set of constituent systems. One would hope the human systems and engineered systems that support the human communities would be designed toward common outcomes and measures. In practice this seldom occurs, particularly with urban infrastructure. While the need for efficiency and scale drive city infrastructure development, the inherent vulnerability, resilience, and sustainability of human communities allows the city to withstand and recover from shocks. The disciplines of engineering and the social sciences rarely come together to address these equally, except on occasion to address natural disasters. Shocks to urban communities can be disaster events, but also equally damaging economic, communication, and demographic changes.

Metrics and models do exist to evaluate resilience of both infrastructure and human well-being, but very few research efforts consider their dynamic performance and function working together. This is an area where human social analytics are sorely needed. In this context, SoS principles are most useful to structure representative analytical measures. This paper will not present a survey of community resilience frameworks, as multiple other authors have done that. This paper will use the community resilience framework previously reported by the author and past co-authors [4]-[7] to discuss the SoS principles and associated human social analytics of community resilience.

Section II of the paper introduces the Human SoS concept. Section III briefly discusses the community resilience framework. Section IV uses the Human SoS concept and the community resilience problem to briefly discuss model development. Section V provides an example of the analytics needed.

II. THE SYSTEMS OF SYSTEMS VIEW

Social Systems are the patterns formed by the interrelationships between individuals, groups, and institutions that together form a whole. Sociotechnical Systems are technology-driven systems that involve significant human and social participation, and that participation in turn influences the architecture and design of the technical system. In such systems both the human/social participation and the engineered system co-adapt over time [8]. Human SoS relates to the intentional design of the social systems in conjunction with the design of a larger sociotechnical SoS. Examples are infrastructures, organizations, political systems, and large product/service platforms.

Human SoS demonstrate several consistent patterns that have been studied by a number of authors. These can be generalized into an analysis process to accelerate the stakeholder's and system designer's learning in the domain of Human SoS architecture. The process highlights the SoS characteristics of a complex system architecture and causes the architect to directly experience them in participatory sessions with stakeholders. Table 1 lists the process.

TABLE 1. ARCHITECTURAL ANALYSIS OF A HUMAN SOS.

SoS Perspectives	The tension between perceptions and facts often form the best starting place to understand the behaviors in a Human SoS. Understanding perspectives is a stakeholder research process best informed by talking to stakeholders.
SoS Definition	A process to identify context, SoS boundaries, appropriate scales and constructs, and enablers or barriers that might exist in the context of interest.
Multi-layer Abstractions	Identifying all of the actors at each societal layer and "what they bring with them" - what abstractions would represent primary performance measures of the current SoS and the desired evolution.
SoS Outcomes	Modeling dimensions of the SoS considering system outputs, outcomes (or goals), and the interactions that cause them.
SoS Communication	Identifying information flows that are relevant to decision making in the SoS. This should include transparency (availability to all parts of the system), timeliness (to make decisions), accuracy, and trust.
SoS Implementation	Human SoS have no single mechanisms of control. Behaviors arise from leadership and incentives instead of authority and control. The architect must design interventions that influence change in the SoS.

The process has proven to be particularly useful in understanding and designing the human characteristics of SoS, which we call Human SoS. This is a structured method that walks the participants through selected stakeholder perspectives, helping to define the SoS, building representative abstractions at different layers of the SoS, agreeing on outcomes, understanding flows, and finally designing alternative implementations of the SoS. A defining analysis process in Human SoS is the determination of multi-layer abstractions. Human communities and enterprises are organized into layers, such as individual/group/society structures or enterprise people/process/organizational structures. This is important when designing a Human SoS – success measures often differ at different layers and the relationships between different constructs or abstractions is often a complex model.

III. HUMAN SOS: URBAN COMMUNITY RESILIENCE

Figure 1 represents a conceptual model of human community resilience represented at multiple scales – the lowest being a human capital construct that describes the human components of standard of living (SoL) and subjective well-being (SWB) critical to community populations. The human capital model was derived in the context of urban communities and their built environment and further in the domain of a city with its infrastructure and environment. Previous research developed a complex structured equation model that relates over 130 human capital development measures to measures of critical infrastructure redevelopment [6]. This model is a representative framework to describe most large urban settings in the United States, other contexts would need adjustments to the model.

Human communities and city infrastructure are strongly coupled interdependent SoS, and they cannot successfully be designed using simple indices or optimization of individual components. There is a need to model these systems using complex representations of human and community development, participatory methods that address system complexity to engage communities and planners, and next generation social analytics tools to evaluate predicted, short-term, and long-term effects of resilience building.

A recent National Institute of Standards and Technology report from a workshop on community resilience evaluated seventeen different approaches to measuring community resilience. They found that none of the frameworks could answer two basic questions: "1. How can community leaders know how resilient their community is?" and "2. How can they know if their decisions and investments to improve resilience are making a significant difference?" They also found that a single set of prescriptive measures or indices was unlikely to support neither all types of communities nor all contexts for planning. The subsequent goals were to develop "community resilience metrics or tools that will reliably predict the physical, economic, and social implications (either positive or negative) of community decisions (either active or passive) made with respect to planning, siting, design, construction, operation, protection, maintenance, repair, and restoration of the built environment." [9]

Community leaders need new decisional analysis methods and tools that directly address these two basic questions. These methods and tools must blend the disciplines of participatory design and development with psychology, engineering, and computer science. In order to effectively model community resilience, one must be able to generalize approaches to the context of local community-specific factors. The definition of appropriate context is a stakeholder agreement process. Current state of community development practice recommends reduction into a few simple to understand (by stakeholders) measures. As a result, the

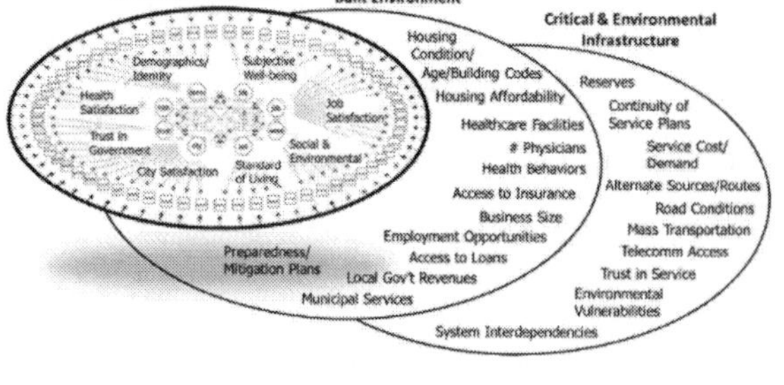

Figure 1. Complex Model of Resilience to Account for Human Capital.

complexity of the environment is lost and the effectiveness of the intervention becomes a debate. In today's era of big data analytics and social network analysis, much richer measures and deeper understanding of results are possible.

Models and measures are needed for optimization of the Human SoS in scenarios and dynamic models that represent both development and collapse of community infrastructure and social constructs (Figure 2). In development scenarios, planners use infrastructure renewal projects and community development to reduce inherent vulnerabilities and build inherent resilience capacity. In disruptive times, crisis response is a reaction to events, development of coping responses is a reinforcement against collapse, and inherent resilience (or sustainability) could be viewed as an attempt to prevent future collapse. The relationship between human capital and shocks are most often represented as a set of capitals that support the coping response of the community [10]-[12]. Example disruptive scenarios are not just natural disasters, they include community gentrification, economic shocks, infrastructure or information collapse, and disaster events. Measures of inherent resilience must address all cases.

IV. Human SoS and Human Analytics Model

Models of the Human SoS and associated analytics support development of decision analysis tools and a multidisciplinary view of community resilience, focused on factors that are known to affect resilience of human populations in areas that are highly dependent on shared infrastructure. Such a toolset would provide a means to integrate often-competing views of infrastructure and community development programs into common outcome measures focused on human community development.

A Human SoS model of resilience must include the social dimensions and the built environment/infrastructure of a community, the constructs that link these together and to long-term community goals, and the plan for both resilience development activities and disaster response. In the SoS context, achievement of resilience is often how well the constituent systems either interact together or fail to do so. Effective gap analysis and understanding of the short and long-term interactions between community and infrastructure development goals, is critical to this process. Measures and models that effectively capture community learning and

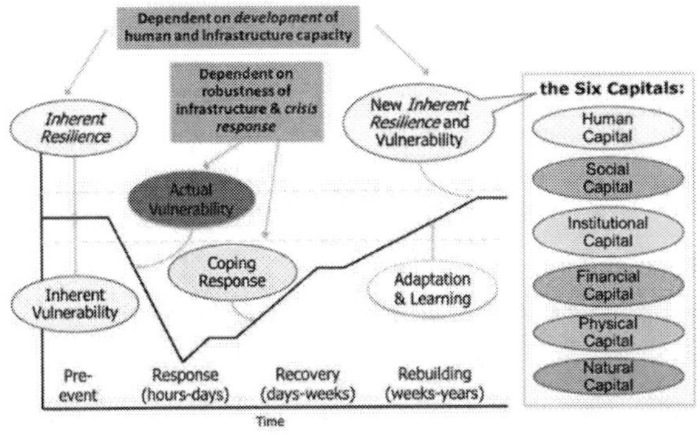

Figure 2: The Dynamic Process of Community Resilience.

likely resilience building outcomes are needed. There is a further need for locally scaled data to be used consistently and appropriately in conjunction with nationally scaled measures supporting national preparedness goals. This is a challenge: finding a consistent set of measurement indicators that are usable by community leaders, but also are valid at local to national scales. Predictive models of community resilience require a much richer selection of qualitative indices and also integration of dynamic models that reflect flows of resources and flows of information.

The conceptualization of a Human SoS modeling and decision support platform would address all of the domains of Figure 3 - conceptual models that reflect model-based analysis of the enterprises under study; data models and datasets that capture both current and future trends; complex system models and simulations to create predictive analyses; and custom visual analytics that allow researchers and policy makers to interact with the data and simulation. The point of Figure 3 is that simple selection and presentation of data does not represent the definition of a Human SoS and an appropriate level of complexity. Human SoS are enterprises and the data must be represented in an appropriate enterprise model that reflect the relationships between data sets and their interdependencies. A second point of Figure 3 is that the collection and curation of data is becoming more prevalent in human settings and the relationship between the enterprise model and the data must be explicit and explanatory. A third point of Figure 3 is that predictive analysis of the data must be incorporated into the appropriate type of computational complex system model based on the purpose of the analysis. This model must use the curated data appropriately. The final point of the Figure is that the communication of the data and the analysis must be in an appropriate visualization form so that the human reviewer can discern the intended patterns. The Human SoS framework helps to consider all of these factors.

We envision the development of such a platform in a community resilience setting as a multidisciplinary activity

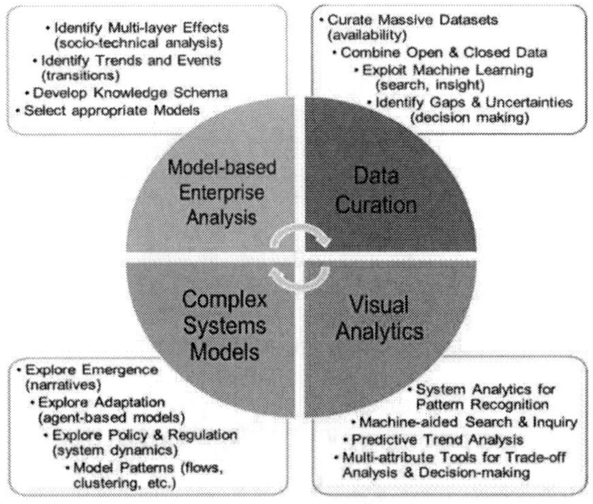

Figure 3: Convergence of Facilitation, Modeling, & Data Analytics Using Modern Software Tools and Methods.

that brings together: 1) Participatory Model Development to engage community stakeholders using a Human SoS architecting methodology, 2) a Complex Model of Human Capital integrated as a decision analysis tool, and 3) a Dynamic Modeling Framework simulating resilience scenarios for predictive analysis and validation using community measured data.

The participatory model development engages with local communities and planners to in a participatory setting using the Human SoS analysis framework of Table 1. The SoS Engineering process would proceed as follows: 1) *SoS Perspectives* involves stakeholder interviews and a conceptual modeling process to identify stakeholders and incentives, the critical interactions in the system that could be used as levers for change, and the measures at different abstraction levels that inform the computational models. 2) The *SoS Definition* is the communities and infrastructure of a city. Models, data, and evaluation research would be bounded to focus specific neighborhoods in the city based on their differing physical characteristics, demographics and social characteristics, and planned development goals and timelines. 3) *Multi-Layer Abstractions* are collected as a set of measurements at representative local and broader scales. 4) *SoS Outcomes* are the respective purpose, goals, and strategies of the systems as envisioned by the stakeholders. These represent intents when embarking on programs to change the systems. 5) *SoS Communication* models the relationships and flows across the defined city resilience model. In this model, the dynamic process of resilience is placed into a model that could capture the representative process relationships and identify measurement points. 6) *SoS Implementation* is a representative model of the technical, economic, and social factors representing the SoS.

These factors come together in a set of complex decision models. It is unlikely that a single model will be able to represent the full complexity of an urban community, but capturing the correct set of dependencies as an SoS model will help to identify emergence (intended or unintended) that arises from combinations of change programs. Over time, this work envisions a tool that policy makers can use that will quickly reveal how changes in funding or resources may impact community resiliency. Such a tool would have an easy-to-use graphical user interface allowing policy holders - regardless of their statistical or programming backgrounds - to understand trends in human capital and community resiliency in an effort to better predict how changes in community resources will impact communities as a whole. Such a tool should include an explorable model of the Human SoS constructs so users can see for themselves the underlying structure of community resiliency. It should also generate trending measures and maps revealing community resiliency at a local and national level. The tool should provide users with valuable information about the statistical and analytical procedures used to create the models in an effort to make the models as transparent and easily communicable as possible. Ideally, policy makers will be able to use this tool in order to make more informed decisions about how to allocate funding or improve communities in a resiliency context.

V. HUMAN SOCIAL ANALYTICS EXAMPLE

Hollnagel describes resilience in systems as being able to respond appropriately to both disturbances and opportunities. He further defines resilience not just as properties of a system, but as its resulting performance [13]. Programs that attempt renewal of infrastructure or community assets should address these as opportunities to increase the resilience of the community as defined by the activities and services provided by and to the human occupants of the community. Figure 4 shows the complex relationships between the objects and processes that define a city. One might consider the input to be the city infrastructure networks that provide services supporting the livelihood of the communities, and the output to be the development of human capital that provides for sustainable and resilient livelihoods of the cities occupants.

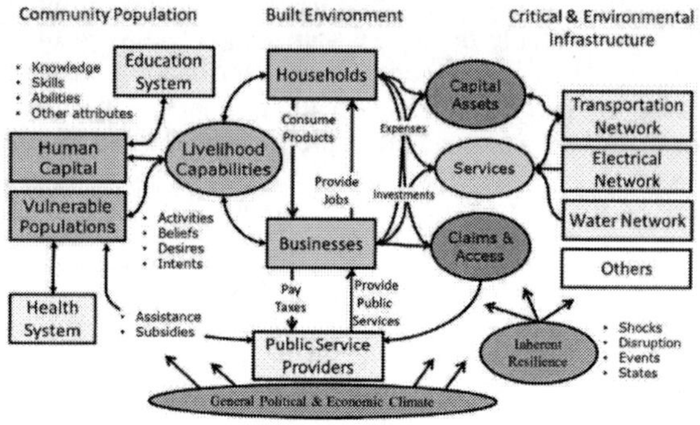

Figure 4: Architecture of a City Representing the Relationships Between Infrastructure, Built Environment, and Community Populations.

A complex model might consider the regentrification of a set of neighborhoods via investment in new city infrastructure and built environment. This development would include support to vulnerable populations with improvements to assisted living for the aging and disabled as well as improved overall community access to healthcare. Tables 2 and 3 list several factors associated with infrastructure, built environment, and human capital that should be considered when addressing community healthcare. Table 2 lists the viewpoints of the city planners, while Table 3 identifies the related human capital components.

TABLE 2. URBAN SOS MODEL OF HEALTH AND ACCESS TO HEALTHCARE.

Model Component	Factor
Housing for Vulnerable Groups	Public shelter capacity
	Age of structures (year built/building codes)
	Housing burden (housing cost/income)
Energy Services	Availabilty (average down times)
	Energy burden (total cost of energy/income)
Health Management	Medical facilities and practitioners
Accessibility	Access to transportation
	Access to communications
Land Use	Parks and recreational facilities

TABLE 3. HUMAN SOS MODEL OF HEALTH AND ACCESS TO HEALTHCARE.

Model Component	Factor
Standard of Living	Physical health condition
	Need for public transit vs. access
	Income
Subjective Wellbeing	Subjective satisfaction with physical health
	Subjective satisfaction with city
Security Climate	Afraid to walk in neighborhood at night
Political Climate	Opinion of gov't spending on healthcare
	Opinion of gov't spending on mass transit
Demographics	Size of city

In the human social analytics domain, monitoring of individuals health condition, as well as their access to healthcare and medical facilities is possible. Poor health is a social vulnerability that will impact the resilience of the human community to shocks. The model above identifies a number of areas of monitoring: access to housing and energy, actual health condition, satisfaction with health, ability to get to medical treatment facilities, and assessment of the city in terms of ability to gain exercise.

Measurements of the built environment and infrastructure are long-term and medium term indicators that would be reflected in a city planning dataset that is maintained year-to-year and adjusted based on the age of the neighborhoods and changing land use patterns. Medium term measures like housing and energy burdens reflect economic conditions that should be tracked regularly and fed into planning activities. The primary challenges with these measures are collection and maintenance of the data at city scales.

Likewise, satisfaction with health and city as well as political climate are factors that should be surveyed and monitored in the medium to long-term at individual and community scales. For the other factors, the availability of social media data, wearables, mobile location data, and other community sensors provide opportunity for near real-time analysis of community patterns. These would include individual monitoring of health vulnerabilities, patterns of mobility, and routine use of wellness opportunities such as parks and recreation. Neighborhoods with lower health indices can be targeted for improvement as well as monitored in response situations.

Putting together a monitoring system that tracks near real-time resilience indices for communities that have varying human capital concerns is possible given priorities and a well-constructed human SoS architecture. It is critical that such a model be defined so that the effectiveness and long-term validation of health capital development programs can be tracked. The complexity of this model should also not be underestimated, but the future of human social analytics needs to be placed in a framework that adequately reflects the complexity of these Human SoS. This paper discusses a framework for development of these models.

VI. CONCLUSIONS

The exploration of the human characteristics of SoS over time led to the development of a framework for SoS analysis that captures purely human outcomes. We call this Human SoS. Key to the analysis is a set of six processes that encourage systems thinking and model development with respect to the human communities that use these systems. These are SoS Perspectives, SoS Definition, Multi-layer Abstractions, SoS Outcomes, SoS Communication, and SoS Implementation. We have evaluated and tested these processes in a number of studies, primarily focused on community resilience, but also in other contexts such as organizational skill retention and political corruption.

The complexity and social adaptation represented in collaborative SoS make the decision space nearly impossible to navigate without a combination of participatory stakeholder driven analysis tools and extensive modeling and simulation. The hope is that the engineering communities, social science communities, and design communities will eventually come together to find common model-based conceptual design approaches that bridge current gaps across disciplines. At this point the community should focus on methods to sense and capture the human analytics that continuously evaluate these metrics.

REFERENCES

[1] Systems Engineering Body of Knowledge (SEBOK), "Systems of Systems (SoS), SEBoK v.1.9, 2017. http://www.sebokwiki.org/wiki/Systems_of_Systems_(SoS) [retrieved: March 2018].

[2] J. H. Holland, "Studying complex adaptive systems," Journal of Systems Science & Complexity, vol.19, no.1, pp. 1–8, 2006.

[3] B. E. White, "On a maturity model for complexity, complex systems, and complex systems engineering," Int. J. of Design & Nature and Ecodynamics, vol. 11, no. 4, pp. 532–542, 2016.

[4] T. McDermott, D. Folds, C. J. Hutto, and M. Nadolski, "A human-focused, holistic model of community resilience," INCOSE Insight, vol. 16, no. 4, December 2016.

[5] C. J. Hutto, "Blending quantitative, qualitative, geospatial, and temporal data: progressing towards the next generation of human social analytics," The Second International Conference on Human and Social Analytics (HUSO 2016), IARIA, Nov. 2016, pp. 48-54, ISBN: 978-1-61208-519-7.

[6] C. J. Hutto, A.a Trani, E. Williams, H. S. Shim, T. McDermott, D. Folds, and M. Nadolski, "The social side of community resilience: human capital modeling," The Third International Conference on Human and Social Analytics (HUSO 2017), IARIA, July 2017, pp. 45-50, ISBN: 978-1-61208-578-4.

[7] T. McDermott and M. Nadolski, "Integrated community resilience, a model based systems engineering approach," INCOSE International Symposium vol. 26, pp. 205-219, 2016.

[8] M. Maier, "Architecting principles for systems of systems," Proceedings of the Sixth Annual International Symposium, INCOSE International Symposium vol. 6, pp. 567-574, 1996.

[9] National Institute of Standards and Technology, NIST GCR 15-993, Community Resilience Workshop, February 2015.

[10] S. Cutter, L. Barnes, M. Berry, C. Burton, E. Evans, E. Tate, and J. Webb, "A place-based model for understanding community resilience to natural disasters," Global Environmental Change, vol. 18, pp. 598-606, 2008.

[11] ARUP & Rockefeller Foundation, City Resilience Index, Research Report Vol. 1, Ove Arup & Partners International Limited, 2014.

[12] United Nations (UNODC), Sustainable Livelihoods: A Broader Vision, Discussion Paper, 2011.

[13] E. Hollnagel, "Resilience engineering," http://erikhollnagel.com/ideas/resilience-engineering.html, [retrieved: April 2018].

A Method for Engineering Resilient Organizational Workforce Systems

simpathē :: Systems Integration of Manpower, Personnel, and Training for HSI Evaluations

Clayton J. Hutto
Human Systems Engineering Branch
Georgia Tech Research Institute (GTRI)
Atlanta, Georgia, USA
e-mail: cjhutto@gatech.edu

Dennis J. Folds
Lowell Scientific Enterprises
Carrollton, GA 30116 USA
e-mail: dennis.folds@gmail.com

***Abstract*—At its core, *resilience* refers to the ability to resist and/or respond to a shock (internal or external stressor, disruption, disturbance, or challenge), and recover from the event once it has occurred. Organizations are complex adaptive systems whose capacity for resilience is embedded in a set of individual-level Knowledge, Skills, Abilities, and Other attributes (KSAOs), as well as a blend of organizational system-level cognitive, behavioral, and contextual capabilities. This paper applies complex systems theory and a Human Systems Integration (HSI) perspective to present a conceptual approach and computational model called *simpathē* (an acronym for Systems Integration of Manpower, Personnel, and Training for HSI Evaluations). The *simpathē* model aims to help assess organizational workforce resilience in two ways: first, it facilitates planning and preparations to help build organizational capacity to resist undesirable effects from system shocks; second, it enables rapid workforce trade-space evaluations to aid in developing situation-specific responses (and ultimately, transformative activities) that capitalize on disruptive events. This paper illustrates the *simpathē* model with a use case example that characterizes organizational workforce resilience in the face of a major technological perturbation within the system—namely, the large-scale (organization-wide) conversion to operating and maintaining a collection of new communication technologies.**

Keywords-organizational resilience; workforce; human systems integration; systems thinking; complex adaptive systems.

I. INTRODUCTION

The nature of change and uncertainty in the environment surrounding businesses associated with health, defense, crisis management and emergency services constantly challenges the resilience of organizations in these industries. Rapidly changing technology, intense competition, the stress of constantly having to do more with less, not to mention the need to be prepared for and respond to natural disasters, pandemic diseases, terrorist attacks or other man-made calamities, economic recessions, safety/security threats, equipment failures and general human errors are just some examples of how many different types of shocks can undermine the stability and security of an organizational system [1]. An organization's workforce—i.e., the resource pool of individuals engaged in or available for work—comprises a major nexus of resilience potential for organizations. Having appropriate numbers of people who possess the appropriate knowledge, skills, and attitudes to operate efficiently and effectively is critical to an organization's capacity to adapt to constant change, respond rapidly and adequately to organizational shocks, and thrive in dynamic and sometimes turbulent environments.

This paper leverages theories and concepts from industrial/organizational psychology, ecology, industrial systems engineering, operations research and management, complexity science, and Human Systems Integration (HSI). It then combines them with resilience research to develop a method for characterizing organizational workforce resilience as a function of interdependencies between *manpower* (the number of people available for work), *personnel* (the aptitudes of the people who work), and the *training* needed to prepare those people to perform the work.

The rest of this paper is organized as follows. Section II presents background and related research that briefly reviews the foundational theory, principles, and concepts employed in this research effort. Section III describes the technical methods for characterizing organizational workforce resilience, while Section IV introduces *simpathē*, a computational model that implements those methods. Section V closes with a use case example to demonstrate how *simpathē* can provide insights and solutions to organizational decision makers for both planning/preparation (i.e., static resilience) and for response/recovery (dynamic resilience).

II. BACKGROUND AND RELATED WORK

Recent years have seen a surge in resilience related research [2]. A considerable amount of this prior work is grounded in the context of disasters and other traumatic events [3]. Furthermore, much of the work is primarily concerned with understanding resilience from the perspective of either individuals or communities [4], with much less emphasis on understanding or characterizing resilience for sociotechnical systems at the organizational level.

The research effort described in this paper is distinct from the (albeit useful and informative) prior literature in both respects. First, the current work addresses the issue of resilience at a system-level in a unique way (exploring static and dynamic resilience associated with an organizational workforce system). Second, the focus is on a more general and pervasive type of organizational system shock (i.e., technological disruptions affecting an industry or business).

Such distinctions necessitate a brief review of exactly what the term *organizational workforce resilience* means in the this context, as well as what it means to refer to organizations as *complex adaptive systems* when referencing the specific domains of *manpower*, *personnel*, and *training* from the systems engineering sub-discipline known as Human Systems Integration.

A. What is Resilience?

The term *resilience* lends itself to interpretations that have relevance to a variety of research interests ranging from physical science disciplines like metallurgy and materials science, to natural science disciplines like ecology (where Holling's seminal 1973 publication linked the concept with an ecosystem's ability to absorb change and still persist [5]) to social sciences like individual and organizational psychology, and applied sciences like safety engineering [1]. Tracking the evolution of the definition of resilience through the years and across the disciplines gives an idea of the broad impact the concept has had to science in general, and helps shape the understanding of its use in this paper, which pairs it with organizational workforce systems.

Shortly following Holling's initial contribution to the field [5], the ecological literature began to reference two types of resilience: first, "ecological resilience" is consistent with Holling's original definition (the ability to absorb change and still persist after a shock); second, "engineering resilience" deals with the dual processes associated with a) building up *resistance* capacity to potential disruptions *a priori*, and b) enhancing the speed of returning to the pre-existing equilibrium [2][6][7]. As one might infer from the title of this paper, these concepts are important to the current effort.

For at least the past few decades, the economics literature has provided significant social science research contributions to the concept of resilience. In particular, Rose offers useful research from the perspective of economic resilience to natural and man-made disasters (c.f., [8][9]). Rose uses the term "static resilience", which refines the concept of resistance in engineering resilience to incorporate specific consideration for proactively developing the ability for maintaining core functions and performing essential tasks when shocked. Rose also introduced "dynamic resilience" to refer to the speed at which a system returns or bounces-back to a pre-shock state. Regional studies literature on resilience further cultivated the concept by calling attention to an important aspect of dynamic resilience: it is "an adaptive notion [...] characterized by complex non-linear dynamics and an adaptive capacity that enables [systems] to rearrange their internal structure spontaneously" [10].

Progressing to the field of operations research and management, the concept of *organizational resilience* is instantiated as the capacity for an organization to resist shocks (by avoiding organizational breakdowns and failures) and return to a normal state—which may be the original state or some other new desired state [11][12]. Sheffi and Rice further emphasize that a resilient organization should incorporate a strategic initiative to build resilience by (preemptively, continuously) monitoring the organizational state, being sensitive to operations and having well-developed situation awareness, maintaining flexibility to create or reduce redundancy when and where needed [12]. Teixeira and Werther similarly advocate for organizations to be anticipatory responders—to anticipate potential challenges and disturbances and to adaptively adjust prior to a disruption [13]. Consistent with prior research [2], this paper synthesizes the above literature into a characterization of organizational resilience that embraces:

a) the concept of engineering resilience [6][7], with both static and dynamic resilience [8][9],
b) the perspective that organizations comprise complex adaptive systems and processes [10],
c) the notion that a system may "recover" by returning to its original state or to a new desired state [11][12],
d) resilience as a strategic initiative to be proactively evaluate organizational decisions [12], and
e) resilient organizations as anticipatory responders such that adaptation to a new desired state may occur ahead of a disruptive event [13].

With these tenants of organizational resilience in mind, *organizational workforce resilience* further focuses and scopes the current effort to considerations associated with the organization's human capital resources—i.e., the resilience embodied in the organization's staffing, tasking, and training of individuals responsible for the work associated with maintaining core functions and performing essential tasks within the organization. The concept of organizational (workforce) resilience is quite different from notions of individual resilience pervasive in psychology literature. Research in that domain is typically oriented around personal characteristics that serve as protective factors and/or promote a person's capacity to survive, bounce-back, and thrive when faced with adversity and crisis. Examples of factors discussed in psychology research include those related to self-esteem, self-confidence, self-efficacy, loci of control, adaptive coping and problem-solving strategies, flexibility and resourcefulness, personality (including the Big 5 and other ego-resiliency traits), emotional intelligence (including self-awareness and assessment), health, and social relationships (see [14]–[18]). A common misconception of organizational resilience is to perceive it as a sum total of individual capacities to be resilient [19]. However, organizations are complex sociotechnical systems that change and evolve not just based on individual orientations and actions but more so through the interactions that individuals have with each other and from interdependencies among the sub-systems and processes in the organization [20].

Whereas individual resilience is too narrow for the purposes of the current effort, the notion of community resilience is slightly too broad. Research in community resilience typically attends to the connections between neighborhoods and community-level organizations, and between a variety of local and non-governmental groups whose professions necessarily focuses on building and protecting places (e.g., engineers, urban planners, architects), as well as those focused on growing and maintaining healthy people (e.g., health care and public health professionals, emergency responders, social service providers, faith-based specialists, educators, law enforcement, etc.) [4][21]–[23].

A. *What is the Complex Adaptive Systems Perspective?*

The current paper provides a useful link between considering the resilience of individuals and the resilience of an entire community. This link is accomplished by taking an explicit complex adaptive systems perspective grounded in specific technical methods from systems engineering and HSI.

Edson [24] offers a helpfully concise formal definition of complex adaptive systems, with short descriptions of the important characteristics that make the perspective so well-suited for applications in organizational resilience research: *Complex adaptive systems are diverse, interconnected systems that exhibit self-organization (purposeful internal evolution), hierarchy (certainty created through structures that bring order and meaning), emergence (a coherent and integrated dynamic of innovation), and learning (planned application of experience to future events) based on environmental feedback in response to uncertainty* (p. 499).

Thus, a *complex system* is composed of a large number of comparatively simpler parts interacting with each other so that the emergent behavior of the whole is intrinsically difficult to predict based only on the behavior of any single part [25][26]. This is due to the nonlinear interactions, dependencies, and relationships among the parts, as well as between parts and the system's environment. Many complex systems are also *adaptive*, meaning they "respond to their environment and alter their behavior in such a way that they can maintain or improve their function, or so they can 'survive' (that is, continue to persist as organized systems)" [25].

The complex adaptive system perspective is a useful framework for conceptualizing organizational resilience because it captures the tenant of adaptability, as well as the nonlinear relationships between aspects of human capital within the workforce (the number and type of people, their aptitudes, their training), the work environment (workweek demands in terms of the dynamics of situationally dependent tasks required, resource availability, time apportioned), and so on [10][23][27]. The emergent nature of this perspective is in contrast to reductionist approaches, which attempt to understand the system as a whole by study individual pieces in isolation; again, the systems perspective emphasizes that the whole is not equal to the simple sum of its parts.

B. *What is Human Systems Integration (HSI)?*

The International Council on Systems Engineering (INCOSE), the Institute of Electrical and Electronics Engineers Computer Society (IEEE-CS), and the Systems Engineering Research Center (SERC) jointly define Human Systems Integration as an interdisciplinary technical and management process for integrating human considerations with and across all system elements [28]. HSI incorporates the following domains as integration considerations: manpower, personnel, training, human factors engineering, occupational health, safety, habitability, and human survivability. Of these domains, the current effort of engineering organizational workforce resilience is principally concerned with the trade-offs related to manpower, personnel, and training. *Manpower* refers to the number and type of people who operate, maintain, support, and provide training for systems [29]. *Personnel* refers to the human aptitudes (such as knowledge, skills, abilities, attitudes) and experiences required to perform the jobs of operators, maintainers, and support staff [29]. *Training* prepares people to perform the tasks necessary to accomplish organizational goals and objectives [29].

III. CHARACTERIZING WORKFORCE RESILIENCE WITH THE *SIMPATHĒ* MODEL

Workforce resilience is an organization's ability to respond and adapt rapidly to threats posed to its workforce. Organizations that can build resiliency into their human capital are more likely to protect their most valuable resources and maintain continuous operations in the event of a crisis. In general, this paper conceptualizes workforce resilience as a function of the interdependencies between manpower, personnel, training, and the organizational context in terms of core functions and essential tasks. The technical foundation for establishing this context is the task analysis. I refer to this conceptual approach for evaluating aspects of organizational workforce resilience as Systems Integration of Manpower, Personnel, and Training for HSI Evaluations, abbreviated as *simpathē* (pronounced "sympathy").

A. *Task Analysis*

In HSI (from the human factors engineering domain), a task analysis involves the study of how a system goal or objective is accomplished. Task analysis includes a detailed decomposition and description of both manual and mental activities, timing/durations, frequency of occurrence, task divisions of labor and allocation (to some combination of one or more humans and/or technology), potential errors, information requirements (both inputs and outputs), requisite aptitudes for task performance, performance criteria, environmental conditions, and other factors involved in or required for one or more people to perform a given task (see [30] for a more complete list of task analysis elements used for various applications). The term *task* is often used interchangeably with activity or process.

The method presented in this paper relies on a minimum of three specific task analysis elements: hierarchical task list with descriptions, task timing (duration), and task frequency.

1) Task List and Descriptions. System functions (goals, objectives) serve as an initial hierarchical framework for further decomposition of goal-directed, step-by-step list of all essential tasks and activities needed to ensure the organization's core functions can be maintained. Ensure that all collateral duties (especially those particularly relevant for disruptive situations) be incorporated to the extent practical.

2) Timing. For each essential task activity, the task timing (durations) are needed in order to determine the labor requirements for ensuring core functions and essential tasks are maintained during organizational shocks. In the absence of direct observation, task times can be analytically derived using empirically-established human performance equations associated with human perceptual process, information and decision processing, and human body movements. For example, the Hick-Hyman empirical equation depicts motor reaction time (RT) in response to perceiving/processing information and making decisions as a logarithmic function of the number of alternative stimuli and responses. Fitts' Law is an empirical equation for movement time (MT), which describes the logarithmic relationships of distance traveled and required precision with the time to complete discrete movement. When combined, the equations above allow analysts to derive total task times (TT), which account for perceptual delays, decision delays, and movement durations:

$$\mathrm{TT} = a + [\, b * \log_2(N)] + k + [\, c * \log_2(\tfrac{2D}{W})\,] \tag{1}$$

Where: a and b are empirically derived constants to account for perceptual and decision processing; N is the number of choices or attention items; k and c are empirically derived constants to account for times difference of specific body part movement (finger, wrist, arm, foot, etc.); D is distance of movement; W is width of target.

Another analytical method used in industrial and production engineering are Predetermined Motion Time Systems (PMTSs), also referred to as Predetermined Time Standards or Predetermined Time Systems (PTS). Methods-Time Measurement (MTM) is one such system useful for quantifying the amount of time required to perform specific tasks under defined conditions.

Because of the complex adaptive nature of organizational systems, it is often useful to understand the range and distribution of times associated with tasks. The Program Evaluation and Review Technique (PERT) [31] accommodates uncertainty by incorporating timing appraisals based on three point estimates: *optimistic time*: the minimum possible time required to accomplish an activity assuming everything proceeds better than is normally expected or that the task is performed by a highly proficient expert; *pessimistic time*: the maximum possible time required to accomplish an activity, assuming things go awry (excluding major catastrophes) or that the task is performed by an non-proficient novice; and the *most likely time*: the best estimate of the time required to accomplish an activity, assuming everything proceeds as normal or that the task is performed by a typical competent worker. The PERT distribution assigns very small probability to extreme values, and so the Modified PERT distribution introduces a fourth parameter, lambda (γ), that controls the weight of the most likely value in the determination of the mean and helps provide control on how much probability is assigned to tail values of the distribution:

$$\mu_{task} = \frac{a + \gamma b + c}{\gamma + 2} \tag{2}$$

Where: a is the minimum (most optimistic) time; b is the most likely time, c is the maximum (most pessimistic) time; γ is the distribution control parameter that becomes useful when $(b - a)$ and $(c - b)$ are very different magnitudes [32].

3) Frequency. In the absence of empirical data, task frequencies can be estimated or rated. For example, Subject Matter Experts (SMEs) reposnible for performing maintenance on the communications equipment for an organization might provide frequency ratings to estimate how often they typically perform certain maintenance tasks on a single piece of equipment. Ratings may be numerical anchors that represent the levels of granularity appropriate for the analysis, for example:

1 = the task is performed at least annually, but typically not more than twice per year.

2 = the task is performed at least semi-annually, but typically not more than monthly.

3 = the task is performed at least monthly, but typically not more than twice per week.

4 = the task is performed at least twice per week, but typically not more than twice per day.

5 = the task is performed at least twice per day, but typically not more than twice per hour.

6 = the task is performed at least twice per hour, but typically not more than once per minute.

B. Manpower Calculations

Using the data from the task analysis (task list, timing, frequency) in conjunction with information regarding numbers of systems and anticipated work-week labor, we can derive required full-time equivalents (FTEs) needed to maintain an organizations core functionality and essential tasks.

1) Equivalent Man-Week. The EMW equation combines the frequency ratings with the modified PERT times to obtain the estimated weekly labor associated with a particular task. For example, the equivalent weekly proportion for any task with a frequency rating of 1 (task is performed at least annually, but typically not more than twice per year) ranges between 1/52 = 0.01923 and 2/52 = 0.03846, because the frequency is bound between 1 and 2 times per 52 weeks. Thus, the EMW labor requirement for a task that takes 90 minutes, but only gets performed once or at most twice in a year is between 1.7307 minutes and 3.4614 minutes.

$$EMW_{task} = \mu_{task} * eqp_{task} \tag{3}$$

Where: μ_{task} is the task-specific point estimate obtained from the modified PERT equation; eqp_{task} is the task frequency expressed as an equivalent weekly proportion.

2) Full-Time Equivalent. The FTE is obtained by the summing the EMW times for all tasks, and then dividing by prescriptive workweek labor (e.g., a 5 day workweek of 8 hours per day is 40 hours, or 2400 minutes). For large, longer-term rebuilding efforts, individuals cannot sustain overload/overtime schedules. FTE should therefore be scaled with "maximum workload buffers" to account for any proportion of time reserved by a utilization threshold. Typical guidance from the field of Human Factors Engineering *[33]* is to limit human utilization workloads to 75%, which improves organizational workforce (static) resilience.

$$FTE = \frac{\Sigma EMW_{task}}{workweek} * 0.75 \quad (4)$$

C. Personnel

For each of the core functions and essential tasks, a list of requisite KSAOs can be identified. Often, these KSAOs will be bundled together into specific job-roles. The degree to which the duties associated with specific job-roles occupy a person's time interacts with the manpower FTE estimates such that the FTE associated with a particular job-role can be formalized as:

$$FTE_{role} = \frac{\Sigma EMW_{task*role}}{workweek} * 0.75 \quad (5)$$

Additionally, a job-task analysis looks at the fit between the requisite KSAOs needed to accomplish the core functions and essential tasks for an organization versus the KSAOs of the people engaged in or available to perform those tasks. A KSAO mismatch (or "personnel gap") occurs when a task or some set of tasks require specific knowledge, skills, abilities, or other aptitudes that are not possessed by individuals working in the organization.

$$\Delta KSAO = KSAO_r - KSAO_p \quad (6)$$

Where: $KSAO_r$ represents the set of requisite knowledge, skills, abilities, or other aptitudes and $KSAO_p$ represents the set possessed by individuals in the organization's workforce. When ΔKSAO > 0 exists, organizations have a personnel gap. When ΔKSAO < 0 exists, organizations have overqualified personnel, which may lead to labor cost inefficiencies or retention issues. Furthermore, when the manpower and personnel domains interact such that there is a discrepancy between the number of role-specific FTEs required to perform all core functions and essential tasks and the number on hand, then the organization becomes less resilient due to either inefficiency (if over-staffed with too many role-specific FTEs) or inability to maintain organizational core functions (if under-staffed with not enough role-specific FTEs).

D. Training

In the ever changing environment of industry and business, an organization's human capital (employee KSAOs) must be constantly updated to keep pace with change. This is especially the case for the type of emblematic shocks organizations frequently encounter (i.e., responding to rapid changes in technology and marketplace shifts). Oftentimes, such organizational system shocks will necessitate either a) an entirely new set of core functions for the organization, or b) new essential tasks to maintain the *same* core functions, and potentially also c) rendering previous functions and/or tasks obsolete, or d) other adjustments and modifications that affect task timing/duration, frequency, or requisite KSAOs.

In complex adaptive systems like organizations, the training domain interacts (and is interdependent) with the manpower and personnel domains. Organizations can be anticipatory responders by identifying training gaps ahead of the crisis of workforce shortages or obsolescence.

IV. SIMPATHE: COMPUTATIONAL MODEL

The methods and techniques described in Section III for *simpathē* represent the conceptual approach for evaluating the interdependencies between manpower, personnel, training, and organizational context in a systematic and integrated way. A computational model that implements these methods and techniques is also useful to aid in more rapid exploration of the trade-space associated with such (nonlinear, complex) interdependencies. The *simpathē* computational model is available as either a standalone computer program (a script written in the Python programming language), or as an interactive browser-based Jupyter Notebook or JupyterLab application. All implementations allow for programmatic access to the models and techniques, but the Jupyter implementations have additional (non-programmatic) user interface elements that add web forms and control widgets to aid with data importing, exploration, and visualization. For example, analysts can use the browser-based JupyterLab application to select an existing task analysis data file, run the program, and view tabular and graphical summaries for manpower requirements associated with all functions and tasks designated in the task analysis. Optional sub-groupings are enabled as well: manpower requirements by personnel, if roles are designated within the task analysis, by hierarchical function or functional area, or by other desired groupings (for example, see the use case example described in the next section). If data is available regarding the organizational system's existing workforce structure, *simpathē* will also assess any potential manpower (and optionally personnel) mismatches between the human capital resources required according to the task analysis versus what is available in the extant workforce, and likewise presents summaries in interactive tables and graphical formats.

V. USE CASE EXAMPLE: TECHNOLOGICAL DISTRUPTION

The United States military is a national defense oriented organization that precisely meets the criteria of being a complex adaptive system, and decision makers regularly apply resilience-thinking to their organizational decision processes. This organization uses an assortment of specialized communications equipment for a large variety of situations. The organization not only operates these specialized communication devices, they must also conduct much of the maintenance for them. As one might imagine, the technology associated with range of these types of devices is widely varied, and is constantly evolving. Such technological innovations, advances, upgrades, or replacements are the source of disruptions for the organization's MPT situation. In an effort to mitigate the negative impacts on manpower, personnel, and training (MPT) for technological disruptions, the organization used *simpathē* to assess MPT risks and potential courses of (COAs). First, *simpathē* helped summarize the FTE requirements for all functions and tasks associated with the maintenance journeymen, supervisors, and support technician roles for designated levels of maintenance (organization-level versus depot level) for one or more selected types of communications equipment (e.g., radio types X, Y, and Z out of a set of 17 types of hand-held, vehicle mounted, or backpack carried communication devices). These FTE requirements were then compared to the extant MPT situation for over 1,000 different maintenance units within the larger organization such that current over- and under-staffing situations were identified. A range of possible technological changes that affected the maintenance functions and tasks were next assessed for their impact on the number and types of maintainers, their aptitudes, and their training. For example, some innovations made KSAOs related to analog communications less applicable, stressing aptitudes related to digital, satellite, and wired/wireless networking KSAOs.

References

[1] R. Bhamra, S. Dani, and K. Burnard, "Resilience: the concept, a literature review and future directions," *Int. J. Prod. Res.*, vol. 49, no. 18, pp. 5375–5393, Sep. 2011.

[2] A. Annarelli and F. Nonino, "Strategic and operational management of organizational resilience: Current state of research and future directions," *Omega*, vol. 62, pp. 1–18, Jul. 2016.

[3] J. Madrigano, A. Chandra, T. Costigan, and J. Acosta, "Beyond Disaster Preparedness: Building a Resilience-Oriented Workforce for the Future," *Int. J. Environ. Res. Public. Health*, vol. 14, no. 12, p. 1563, Dec. 2017.

[4] A. Chandra *et al.*, *Understanding Community Resilience in the Context of National Health Security: A Literature Review*. RAND Corporation, 2010.

[5] C. Holling, "Resilience and Stability of Ecological Systems," *Annu. Rev. Ecol. Syst.*, vol. 4, no. 1, pp. 1–23, Nov. 1973.

[6] E. Hollnagel, D. D. Woods, and N. Leveson, Eds., *Resilience engineering: concepts and precepts*. Aldershot, England; Burlington, VT: Ashgate, 2006.

[7] L. T. T. Dinh, H. Pasman, X. Gao, and M. S. Mannan, "Resilience engineering of industrial processes: Principles and contributing factors," *J. Loss Prev. Process Ind.*, vol. 25, no. 2, pp. 233–241, Mar. 2012.

[8] A. Rose, "Defining and measuring economic resilience to disasters," *Disaster Prev. Manag. Int. J.*, vol. 13, no. 4, pp. 307–314, Sep. 2004.

[9] A. Rose, "Economic resilience to natural and man-made disasters: Multidisciplinary origins & contextual dimensions," *Environ. Hazards*, vol. 7, no. 4, pp. 383–398, 2007.

[10] G. Bristow and A. Healy, "Regional Resilience: An Agency Perspective," *Reg. Stud.*, vol. 48, no. 5, pp. 923–935, 2014.

[11] H. Carvalho, V. C. Machado, and J. G. Tavares, "A mapping framework for assessing supply shain resilience," *Int. J. Logist. Syst. Manag.*, vol. 12, no. 3, p. 354, 2012.

[12] Y. Sheffi and J. B. Rice, "A Supply Chain View of the Resilient Enterprise," *MIT Sloan Manag. Rev.*, vol. 47, no. 1, pp. 41–48, Sep. 2005.

[13] E. de O. Teixeira and W. B. Werther, "Resilience: Continuous renewal of competitive advantages," *Bus. Horiz.*, vol. 56, no. 3, pp. 333–342, May 2013.

[14] A. S. Masten, "Ordinary magic. Resilience processes in development," *Am. Psychol.*, vol. 56, no. 3, pp. 227–238, 2001.

[15] A. D. Ong, C. S. Bergeman, and S. M. Boker, "Resilience Comes of Age: Defining Features in Later Adulthood," *J. Pers.*, vol. 77, no. 6, pp. 1777–1804, Dec. 2009.

[16] L. V. Polk, "Toward a middle-range theory of resilience," *ANS Adv. Nurs. Sci.*, vol. 19, no. 3, pp. 1–13, Mar. 1997.

[17] G. E. Richardson, "The metatheory of resilience and resiliency," *J. Clin. Psychol.*, vol. 58, no. 3, pp. 307–321, Mar. 2002.

[18] M. M. Tugade and B. L. Fredrickson, "Resilient Individuals Use Positive Emotions to Bounce Back From Negative Emotional Experiences.," *J. Pers. Soc. Psychol.*, vol. 86, no. 2, pp. 320–333, 2004.

[19] D. P. Ashmos and G. P. Huber, "The Systems Paradigm in Organization Theory: Correcting the Record and Suggesting the Future," *Acad. Manage. Rev.*, vol. 12, no. 4, pp. 607–621, Oct. 1987.

[20] C. A. Lengnick-Hall, T. E. Beck, and M. L. Lengnick-Hall, "Developing a capacity for organizational resilience through strategic human resource management," *Hum. Resour. Manag. Rev.*, vol. 21, no. 3, pp. 243–255, Sep. 2011.

[21] A. Chandra *et al.*, "Getting actionable about community resilience: the Los Angeles County Community Disaster Resilience project," *Am. J. Public Health*, vol. 103, no. 7, pp. 1181–1189, Jul. 2013.

[22] A. Chandra *et al.*, "Building Community Resilience to Disasters: A Way Forward to Enhance National Health Security," *Rand Health Q.*, vol. 1, no. 1, p. 6, 2011.

[23] J. Acosta, A. Chandra, and J. Madrigano, *An Agenda to Advance Integrative Resilience Research and Practice*. Santa Monica, CA, USA: RAND Corporation, 2017.

[24] M. C. Edson, "A Complex Adaptive Systems View of Resilience in a Project Team: Resilience in a Project Team," *Syst. Res. Behav. Sci.*, vol. 29, no. 5, pp. 499–516, Sep. 2012.

[25] B. MacLennan, "Evolutionary Psychology, Complex Systems, and Social Theory," *Sound. Interdiscip. J.*, vol. 90, no. 3, pp. 169–189, 2007.

[26] R. J. Eidelson, "Complex adaptive systems in the behavioral and social sciences.," *Rev. Gen. Psychol.*, vol. 1, no. 1, pp. 42–71, 1997.

[27] G. Bristow and A. Healy, "Building Resilient Regions: Complex Adaptive Systems and the Role of Policy Intervention," *Raumforsch. Raumordn.*, vol. 72, no. 2, pp. 93–102, Apr. 2014.

[28] R. D. Adcock, Ed., *Guide to the Systems Engineering Body of Knowledge (SEBoK)*, V. 1.9. International Council on Systems Engineering (INCOSE), Institute of Electrical and Electronics Engineers Computer Society (IEEE-CS), Systems Engineering Research Center (SERC), 2017.

[29] National Research Council, *Human-System Integration in the System Development Process: A New Look*. Washington, D.C.: National Academies Press, 2007.

[30] B. Kirwan and L. Ainsworth, *A Guide To Task Analysis: The Task Analysis Working Group*. Philadelphia, PA, USA: Taylor & Francis, 1992.

[31] D. G. Malcolm, J. H. Roseboom, C. E. Clark, and W. Fazar, "Application of a Technique for Research and Development Program Evaluation," *Oper. Res.*, vol. 7, no. 5, pp. 646–669, Oct. 1959.

[32] D. Vose, *Risk analysis: a quantitative guide*, 3rd ed. Hoboken, NJ: Wiley, 2008.

[33] S. G. Charlton and T. G. O'Brien, Eds., *Handbook of human factors testing and evaluation*, 2nd ed. Mahwah, N.J: Lawrence Erlbaum Associates, Publishers, 2002.

An Approach to Web Adaptation by Modelling User Interests Using TF-IDF: A Feature Selection and Multi-Criteria Approach Using AHP

Dimitris K. Kardaras
School of Business, Athens University of Economics and Business,
Athens, Greece
email: kardaras@aueb.gr

Ilias Petrounias
The University of Manchester, Oxford Rd M13 9PL,
Manchester, UK
email: ilias.petrounias@manchester.ac.uk

Stavroula Barbounaki
Merchant Marine Academy of Aspropyrgos,
Athens, Greece
email: sbarbounaki@yahoo.gr

Stavros Kaperonis
Panteion University of Social and Political Sciences,
Athens, Greece
email: skap@panteion.gr

***Abstract*—User reviews provide a rich source of information regarding user interests. Many Web platforms allow or even encourage their visitors to leave their feedback regarding the products and services they have consumed. The Term Frequency (TF) and the Inverse Document Frequency (IDF) are two factors that have been used extensively in capturing users' preferences. This paper collects users' reviews from e-tourism Web platforms, calculates the TF and the IDF for each user and adopts a multi-criteria approach in order to quantify users' preferences and dynamically adapt the websites design accordingly. It utilizes the Analytic Hierarchy Process (AHP) and similarity methods in order to determine the relative importance of terms and Web pages and then rearranges them in a new website structure.**

Keywords-Web Adaptation; TF-IDF; AHP; Multi-Criteria Analysis.

I. INTRODUCTION

According to the Internet Web statistics, there are approximately 7,634,758,428 Web users around the globe [1]. Data also shows that more than 1.5 billion websites exist today, with more 200 million being active [2]. A great number of Web users often leave their feedback in the form of users' reviews, thus developing a very rich source of information regarding services and products, customers' needs and suppliers' quality. Thus, a huge amount of information becomes available to users for almost every single topic. Although this is a very promising development, at the same time searching through this vast ocean of data in order to identify the required information is quite of an endeavour. Within the context of Web personalisation, context personalisation aims at providing the right information to the right user, while presentation personalisation focuses on presenting the content with the most suitable media combination taking into account users' factors such as media limitations, users' media preferences, etc [3]. With respect to presentation personalisation, [3] suggest 5 groups of factors to be taken into consideration:

User-specific features pertain to users' media preferences. For example, a user would rather choose a graphical to text presentation. *Information features* refer to representational differences and capabilities of media since not all media are equally suitable for projecting the same piece of information. *Contextual information* refers to user environmental conditions, such as noise, light, weather, speed, etc. that may affect the presentation quality to the user. *Media constraints* imply the need to effectively combine the characteristics and capabilities of different media in order to improve the quality of presentation. *Limitations of technical resources* relate to device limitations such as screen size, bandwidth, etc. With respect to content personalisation, the analysis of User Generated Content (UGC) provides Web developers as well as service and product designers with valuable information regarding users' preferences as well as suppliers quality and potential [4]. The Term Frequency (TF) and the Inverse Document Frequency (IDF) are used extensively in capturing user preferences [5]. Several representational methodologies have been proposed for developing user profiles. Most frequently though are the three different formats namely: *keywords*, *semantic networks* and *concept-based* representations [5][6]. Keywords represent domains of users' preferences. They are associated with weights that indicate the strength of user interests for a particular topic. Polysemy and Synonymy are problems associated with keywords. Semantic networks, address these problems, by representing keywords with nodes on graphs that are connected with each other, including co-occurrences. Concept-based representations resemble semantic networks in structure but they differ in having nodes to represent abstract topics rather than keywords [5][6]. Filtering and clustering techniques are very useful in reducing the number of concepts that are found on the Web when attempting to formulate user profiles. However, [6] argues that these techniques lack effectiveness for they produce the same structure of user preferences for users with different needs, thus failing to produce highly refine, accurate and personalised representations of individual users. Research shows that while many approaches have been used in order to produce and use user profiles, e.g. in Web personalisation, recommender systems, etc., there exists no definite procedure for deriving user interests [6][7]. The AHP have been used in documents ranking [8]. However, the use of multi-criteria methods in analysing the TF-IDF is overlooked. This paper addresses the need for investigating alternative ways of developing user preferences models and suggests the analysis of the TF-IDF with the use of AHP.

Thus, this research aims to propose a multi-criteria approach based on the AHP and the TF-IDF for adapting websites design according to users' preferences relative importance. The relative importance of users' interests has not been considered in the literature. When it comes to personalisation though, it is the relative importance of terms for each individual user that would rank and distinguish users' interests and subsequently decide how to structure websites. Web adaptation is a decision making process where users would pairwise compare terms and decide which ones they mostly prefer to know about. Their choices influence the Web design, which needs to adapt to users' preferences. The rest of the paper is structured as follows. Section II presents the proposed methodology and the methods used for data analysis. In Section III, the paper discusses the empirical study and the data analysis. Finally, the paper presents its conclusions in Section IV.

II. Methodology and Methods

This paper aims to dynamically rearrange the structure of websites, according to user interests. By capturing and modelling user preferences, this paper proposes an approach to reallocate Web pages based on their importance. Web pages' importance is calculated based on user priorities. Data is collected from platforms such as TripAdvisor.com and Booking.com. User reviews, regarding users' stay in Greece and Italy hotels, were collected by using the Scrapy Web crawler tool. The reviews were then analysed by utilizing the Knime text mining tool. Next, the importance of each term was calculated and analysed by utilizing the Analytic Hierarchy Process (AHP) multicriteria analysis method. In recent years, many researchers adopted Multi-Criteria Decision Making (MCDM) approaches to problem solving such assessing alternative solutions, to selection problems, strategic analysis [9] etc. The steps of the proposed methodology adopted follow.

A. *Methodology for evaluating business strategy based on Web analytics.*

Step 1: Collect documents published by users.

A total of 5453 reviews were collected, from hotels ranging from 3 to 5 stars. The data size is more than sufficient for calculating user preferences with AHP. Reviews were analysed in order to calculate the Term Frequency (TF) and the Inverse Document Frequency (IDF) factors.

Step 2: Calculate the importance W_{tk} for each term (t_k) and formulate User-Interests Vector (UIV). Calculate the importance of each term (t_k), using the following formula:

$$W_{tk} = TF_{tk} * IDF_{tk} \quad (1)$$

where, W_{tk}, represents the weight of term (t_k), TF_{tk}, is the term frequency for term (t_k), $IDF_{tk} = \log(\frac{N_u}{d_{tk}})$, N_u, is the total number of documents published by user (u) and d_{tk}, represents the number of documents that contain term (t_k). The UIV shows the importance that each user perceives for each term. The UIV takes the following from: $UIV_u^n = \{w_{(u,1)}, w_{(u,2)}, \dots, w_{(u,k)}\}$. Thus, $UIV = \{w_{(u,t)}\}$, where $w_{(u,t)}$ indicates the weight, i.e. the importance of term ($t = 1,..k$) for user ($u = 1,..n$). By combining all users' preferences, the UIM matrix is formed.

$$UIM_u^n = \begin{matrix} w_{(1,1)} & w_{(1,2)} & w_{(1,3)} & \dots & w_{(1,k)} \\ w_{(2,1)} & w_{(2,2)} & w_{(2,3)} & \dots & w_{(2,k)} \\ w_{(3,1)} & w_{(3,2)} & w_{(3,3)} & \dots & w_{(3,k)} \\ \dots & \dots & \dots & \dots & \dots \\ w_{(n,1)} & w_{(n,2)} & w_{(n,3)} & \dots & w_{(n,k)} \end{matrix}$$

Each row of the *UIM* matrix represents the preferences of the user associated with the corresponding. The UIM will later be used to calculate the interests' similarities among users and recommend users items to see.

Step 3: Evaluate the relative importance of each Web page for every user using AHP.

Each Web page is assessed in terms of the importance of the terms it contains. Drawing on each user's UIV, the AHP pairwise comparison matrix is calculated. The pairwise comparison matrix that shows terms' perceived importance for each user takes the following form.

$$A^u = \begin{matrix} & t_1 & t_2 & \dots & t_k \\ t_1 & 1 & a^u{}_{(1,2)} & \dots & a^u{}_{(1,k)} \\ t_2 & 1/a^u{}_{(1,2)} & 1 & \dots & a^u{}_{(2,k)} \\ \dots & \dots & \dots & 1 & \dots \\ t_k & 1/a^u{}_{(1,k)} & 1/a^u{}_{(2,k)} & \dots & 1 \end{matrix},$$

where $a^u{}_{(i,j)} = {w_{(u,i)}}/{w_{(u,j)}}$, $\forall i, j = \{1,..., k\}$ with i and j indicating the terms and $and \forall u = \{1,...n\}$, where u, indicates the users. If $i = j$ then $a^u{}_{(i,j)} = 1$.

In order to proceed with the AHP, assume the following hierarchy:

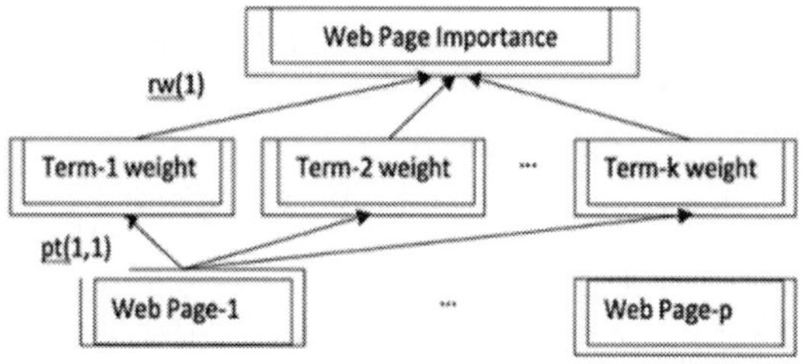

Figure 1: The AHP hierarchy for the evaluation of Web pages relative importance

The terms relative importance for each user reflects Web pages importance for each user, since a Web page is a collection of terms. Thus, the AHP analysis returns the relative importance of each term; therefore, the relative weight of each Web page for each user. A Web page is modelled as a vector which elements are the relative importance $rw_{(t)}$ of each term as resulted from the AHP, weighted by the normalised frequency ($pt_{wp,tk}$) that term t_k appears on the corresponding Web page ($wp = 1,...p$). Time related factors can also be used in measuring Web pages importance. Thus, drawing on the AHP theory, the importance of every Web page is represented by the *User Page Vector* (UPV) as follows:

$$UPV^p_{wp} = \{rw_{(t1)} * pt_{(wp,t1)}, rw_{(t2)} * pt_{(wp,t2)}, ..., rw_{(tk)} * pt_{wp,tk}\} = \{upv^p{}_{t1}, upv^p{}_{t2}, ...upv^p{}_{tk}\} \quad (2)$$

where, $\sum_{tk=1}^{k} pt_{wp,tk} = 1$ since frequencies are normalised and $upv^p{}_{tk} = rw_{(ti)} * pt_{(wp,ti)}$ Indicating the importance of term t_k in page *wp*. If a term does not appear on a Web page (i.e. $pt_{wp,tk} = 0$) then the term's importance for the corresponding page is zero.

Step 4: website Modelling. By considering the UPV^p_{wp} of all Web pages in a website, the *User Site Matrix* (USM) is formed. Thus, $USM = \{UPV_{(p)}\}$ .The USM matrix takes the following form:

$$USM^u = \begin{matrix} UPV^u{}_1 \\ UPV^u{}_2 \\ \cdots \\ UPV^u{}_{wp} \end{matrix}, \forall wp = 1,...p,$$

where *wp* indicates the Web pages, $\forall u = \{1,...n\}$, and *u* indicating the users.

Step 5: Calculate the Similarity of Web Pages. Drawing on the USM matrix, the similarity between Web pages is calculated by using the following formula of the cosine similarity method.

$$s_{i,j} = \frac{\left|\sum_{i,j=1,u=1}^{p,n} upv_{iu} * upv_{ju}\right|}{\sqrt{\left(\sum_{i,j=1,u=1}^{p,n} upv^2_{iu}\right) * \left(\sum_{i,j=1,u=1}^{p,n} upv^2_{ju}\right)}} \quad (3)$$

where $u = 1,..n$ and $i, j = 1,2,..., p$ representing users and Web pages respectively. Web pages with high similarity values are re-grouped in website layers.

Step 6: Rearrange Web pages into website layers (L). The total number of Web pages (P) in a website is calculated by using the following formula:

$$P = \frac{T}{tpp}, \quad (4)$$

where *P*, is the total number of Web pages in a website; *T* indicates the total number of terms identified and *tpp*, is the number of terms allowed per page. The resulting number *P* is round up to the next integer if needed.

Next, assume the allowed number of Web Pages per Layer (WPL) in the website and calculate the number of required website layers (L), by using the following formula:

$$L = \frac{P}{wpl}, \quad (5)$$

where *L* is the total number of layers in a website; *P*, is the total number of Web pages in a website and *wpl* is the allowed number of Web pages per layer. The resulting number *L* is round up to the next integer if needed.

Web pages of similar importance are grouped together into the layers. Therefore, a layer $L_{WL} = \{WP_i, WP_j, ...WP_p\}$, where L_{WL} is the WL-th website layer, which consists of a group of Web pages

$WP_i, WP_j, ...WP_p$, where $i, j, p = 1,2,..., p$. The Web pages are grouped upon their importance similarity degree.

B. *The Analytic Hierarchy Process (AHP) Method.*

The AHP method was developed by [10]–[13]. It considers a hierarchy of criteria and possibly sub-criteria that contribute towards the realisation of the goal. The AHP calculates the relative weight of each criterion, i.e. the importance of each criterion with respect to the goal. Upon the criteria hierarchy and their relative importance, the AHP evaluates and ranks a set of alternatives. The AHP and its fuzzy extension [14] have been extensively used in multi-criteria decision making problems [15], such as in selection [16]–[18], strategic management [19], in determining the critical factors of success for information service industry [14], etc. The steps of the AHP are discussed below:

AHP Step 1: Assume a set of criteria which are evaluated in a pairwise manner using a nine point scale [13]. The criteria are represented by the comparison matrix A.

$$A = \begin{matrix} 1 & a_{(1,2)} & a_{(1,3)} & \cdots & a_{(1,n)} \\ 1/a_{(1,2)} & 1 & a_{(2,3)} & \cdots & a_{(2,n)} \\ 1/a_{(1,3)} & 1/a_{(2,3)} & 1 & \cdots & a_{(3,n)} \\ \cdots & \cdots & \cdots & \cdots & \cdots \\ 1/a_{(1,n)} & 1/a_{(2,2n} & 1/a_{(3,n)} & \cdots & 1 \end{matrix}$$

AHP Step 2: The criteria relative weights are calculated by using the formula (6):

$$A * w = \lambda_{\max} * w \qquad (6)$$

where w represents the eigenvector of the matrix A comparison matrix, and $\lambda_{\max}$ is the largest eigenvalue of the matrix A.

AHP Step 3: Calculate the consistency rate.

The consistency of the matrix and subsequently the consistency of the weights is calculated by examining the reliability of judgments in the pairwise comparison. The Consistency Index (CI) and the Consistency Ratio (CR) are defined by using the following formulas:

$$CI - \frac{\lambda_{\max} - n}{n-1} \quad (7) \quad \text{and} \quad CR = \frac{CI}{RI} \quad (8)$$

where n is the number of criteria used in comparison matrix A, and RI is the Random Index. The RI values for a number of criteria (n) are shown in Table 1.

TABLE I. THE RANDOM INDEX (RI)

n	1	2	3	4	5	6	7	8	9
RI	0.00	0.00	0.58	0.90	1.12	1.24	1.32	1.41	1.45

AHP Step 4: Synthesise and Calculate the Alternatives' Evaluation

The evaluation of each alternative is calculated by taking the sum of products of weights by using the following formula:

$$Eal_i = \sum_{i=1}^{m} \prod_{j=1}^{n} w_{i,j} * w_j \qquad (9)$$

where Eal_i indicates the evaluation of alternative (I) is, $i = 1,..m$ indicates the alternatives, $j = 1,..n$ represents the criteria, $w_{i,j}$ is the weight of alternative (i) with respect to criterion (j) and w_j is the weight of the criterion (j).

III. EMPIRICAL STUDY AND DATA ANALYSIS

Assume that for User-1 the total number of documents (N_{u1}=15) and the total number of terms identified in the documents are ($T = 13$). Assume the data shown in Table 2 is collected by analysing User-1 documents. Similar analysis is performed for all users.

TABLE II. TERMS IDENTIFIED FROM USER-1 DOCUMENTS AND ASSOCIATED WEIGHTS

row ID	USER-1 Terms	TF	Term Weight (Wt) Formula (1)
Row2	Hotel furnishing	0.041666667	0.02912375
Row6	Restaurant quality	0.069767442	0.061050786
Row10	bathroom	0.023255814	0.011095843
Row65	Timeliness of service	0.048780488	0.057370305
Row88	terrace	0.037037037	0.032409676
Row91	food	0.037037037	0.025887778
Row700	design	0.037037037	0.017671158
Row42	Quality of coffee	0.00990099	0.003277161
Row951	balcony	0.022222222	0.004929972
Row967	sea	0.022222222	0.010602695
Row995	fruits	0.022222222	0.007355405
Row997	sleep	0.014925373	0.004940197
Row1023	Understanding of staff	0.014925373	0.004940197

The application of the AHP returns the relative weights for each term. The AHP weights are shown in Table 3.

TABLE III. AHP TERMS' RELATIVE WEIGHTS

Terms	AHP Terms weights
furnish	0.106724446
restaurant	0.223721576
bathroom	0.04884162
timeliness	0.210234397
terrace	0.118765775
food	0.094866174
design	0.064756238
coffee	0.012009207
balcony	0.018065962
sea	0.038853743
fruits	0.026953998
sleep	0.018103432
understanding	0.018103432

Next, assume a subset of the terms' frequencies, as shown in Table 4, for each web page. This data is collected by counting the number each term appears on each Web page. For example, the term "furnish" appears 3 times in Web page-1, 5 times in Web page-2, etc.

TABLE IV. THE FREQUENCIES FOR EACH TERM PER WEB PAGE

Terms	Frequencies per Web page				
	Wp-1	*Wp-2*	*Wp-3*	*Wp-4*	*Wp-5*
furnish	3	5	1	0	3
restaurant	1	1	0	1	3
bathroom	3	5	2	1	7

Table 5 shows the normalised frequencies for each term per every page. The normalised frequencies are calculated by dividing each term's frequency of appearance on a web page by the sum of all terms frequencies of appearance on that web page.

TABLE V. TERMS' RELATIVE FREQUENCIES

Terms	Relative Normalised Frequencies per Web page				
	Wp-1	*Wp-2*	*Wp-3*	*Wp-4*	*Wp-5*
furnish	0.103448276	0.151515	0.034483	0	0.103448276
restaurant	0.034482759	0.030303	0	0.045455	0.103448276
bathroom	0.103448276	0.151515	0.068966	0.045455	0.24137931

Next, the importance of each Web page is calculated drawing on the terms' relative normalised frequencies and the terms AHP weights by using formulas (2) and (9). The results are shown in Table 6.

TABLE VI. THE WEB PAGES' IMPORTANCE BASED ON TERMS' RELATIVE IMPORTANCE

	Wp-1	*Wp-2*	*Wp-3*	Wp-4	Wp-5
furnish	0.01104046	0.016170371	0.00368	0	0.01104046
restaurant	0.007714537	0.006779442	0	0.010169	0.023143611
bathroom	0.005052581	0.007400245	0.003368	0.00222	0.011789357
timeliness	0.03624731	0.006370739	0.007249	0.009556	0.007249462
terrace	0.004095372	0.007197926	0.004095	0.005398	0.004095372
food	0.009813742	0.020123128	0.009814	0.008624	0.003271247
design	0.002232974	0.00392462	0.008932	0.014717	0.002232974
coffee	0.000414111	0.001091746	0.001242	0.001638	0.002070553
balcony	0.001868893	0.000547453	0.003115	0.000821	0.000622964
sea	0.004019353	0.003532158	0.006699	0.005298	0.004019353
fruits	0.002788345	0.000816788	0.000929	0.001225	0.000929448
sleep	0.000624256	0.000548589	0.001249	0.001646	0.000624256
understanding	0.000624256	0.000548589	0.000624	0.000823	0.000624256
Web pages' importance using formula (9), i.e. sum of terms' weights	**0.086536189**	**0.075051795**	**0.050997**	**0.062136**	**0.071713313**

Drawing on the Web pages relative importance, their similarity is calculated, using formula (3). The similarity degrees are shown in Table 7.

TABLE VII. WEB PAGES IMPORTANCE SIMILARITIES

Similarity Degrees	Wp-1	Wp-2	Wp-3	Wp-4	Wp-5
Wp-1	1	0.618507331	0.662001567	0.627411733	0.568705
Wp-2	0.618507331	1	0.777926514	0.624975126	0.659007
Wp-3	0.662001567	0.777926514	1	0.568704978	0.431098
Wp-4	0.627411733	0.624975126	0.568704978	1	0.623204
Wp-5	0.568704978	0.659006777	0.43109794	0.623203947	1

Drawing on the importance and similarities degrees shown in Tables 6 and 7, respectively, Web pages are grouped into layers. Assuming that the allowed number of terms per page (tpp=2) and total number of terms (T=13), then the maximum number of Web pages is 13/2=6.5 round up to 7, by applying formula (4). By applying formula (5), assuming wpl=2 pages per layer, the maximum number of layers is 7/2, which rounded returns maximum 4 layers in the website. Results show that Web page-1 is the most important followed by Web page-2 and Web page-5. However, Web page-5 is the least important of the three, thus it is arranged in a hierarchical level below in the website, since the maximum number of pages per layer (*wpl*) is set at two (2). Web page-3 is grouped with Web page-2 since the two are more similar than with the other pages. Thus, Web page-3 is linked to Web page-2 but in a layer below, due to (*wpl*) limitation. Similarly, Web page-4 is linked with Web page-1 but following in a layer below. Thus, the resulting website structure is shown in Figure 2.

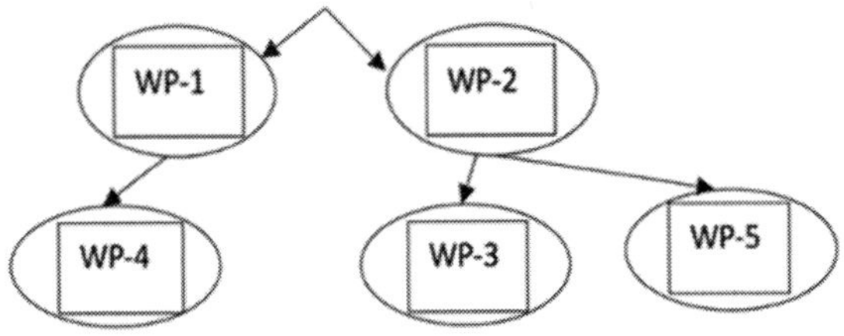

Figure 2: The resulting Web structure

In the same way, similarities among terms are calculated so that terms are re-arranged accordingly, i.e. to be removed from one page and linked with another. By calculating the similarities between terms and among Web pages, terms can be grouped dynamically and re-grouped so that the content of Web pages changes, thus manipulating the page's importance in a flexible way and produce alternative websites' designs.

IV. CONCLUSIONS

UGC provides a rich source of information regarding user preferences. Content personalisation and presentation personalisation rely on understanding and modelling users' interests. This paper suggests that the use of multi-criteria approaches can be used in conjunction with similarity methods to analyse text indices such as the TF-IDF, etc. The proposed approach utilises the AHP in order to calculate the relative importance of terms and subsequently of the associated Web pages. Upon their importance and similarities terms and Web pages can be re-arranged, thus producing Web structures that dynamically adapt to user preferences following. As soon as user interests' change and these changes can be traced in UGC, the proposed approach recalculates importance and similarity degrees and adapts the Web design. Future research can focus on calculating similarities of users and adopting recommender systems technologies and methods in the Web design domain.

REFERENCES

[1] "Internet Web Stats Web Users," *Internet Web Stats Web Users (2018). https://www.internetworldstats.com/stats.htm, Last viewed 10/5/2018.*, 2018. [Online]. Available: https://www.internetworldstats.com/stats.htm.

[2] "Internet Web Stats websites (2018)," *Internet Web Stats websites (2018). http://www.internetlivestats.com/total-number-of-websites/, Last viewed 10/5/2018.*, 2018. .

[3] A. Bunt, G. Carenini, and C. Conati, "Adaptive content presentation for the web," in *The adaptive web*, Springer, 2007, pp. 409–432.

[4] V. Baka, "The becoming of user-generated reviews: Looking at the past to understand the future of managing reputation in the travel sector," *Tour. Manag.*, vol. 53, pp. 148–162, 2016.

[5] A. Hawalah and M. Fasli, "Dynamic user profiles for web personalisation," *Expert Syst. Appl.*, vol. 42, no. 5, pp. 2547–2569, 2015.

[6] S. Saleheen and W. Lai, "UIWGViz: An architecture of user interest-based web graph vizualization," *J. Vis. Lang. Comput.*, vol. 44, pp. 39–57, 2018.

[7] B. Magnini and C. Strapparava, "Improving user modelling with content-based techniques," in *International Conference on User Modeling*, 2001, pp. 74–83.

[8] A. I. El-Dsouky, H. A. Ali, and R. S. Rashed, "Ranking Documents Based on the Semantic Relations Using Analytical Hierarchy Process," *Int. J. Adv. Comput. Sci. Appl.*, vol. 7, no. 2, pp. 164–173, 2016.

[9] N. B. Moghaddam, M. Sahafzadeh, A. S. Alavijeh, H. Yousefdehi, and S. H. Hosseini, "Strategic environment analysis using DEMATEL method through systematic approach: Case study of an energy research institute in Iran," *Manag. Sci. Eng.*, vol. 4, no. 4, p. 95, 2010.

[10] T. L. Saaty, "On the measurement of intengibles. A principal eigenvector approach to relative measurement derived from paired comparisons," *Not. Am. Math. Soc.*, vol. 60, no. 2, pp. 192–208, 2013.

[11] T. L. Saaty, *Decision making for leaders: the analytic hierarchy process for decisions in a complex world.* RWS publications, 1990.

[12] T. L. Saaty, "Axiomatic foundation of the analytic hierarchy process," *Manage. Sci.*, vol. 32, no. 7, pp. 841–855, 1986.

[13] T. L. Saaty, "The analytical hierarchy process: planning, setting priorities, resource allocation." McGraw-Hill International Book Co., New York, 1980.

[14] M.-K. Chen and S.-C. Wang, "The critical factors of success for information service industry in developing international market: Using analytic hierarchy process (AHP) approach," *Expert Syst. Appl.*, vol. 37, no. 1, pp. 694–704, 2010.

[15] O. S. Vaidya and S. Kumar, "Analytic hierarchy process: An overview of applications," *Eur. J. Oper. Res.*, vol. 169, no. 1, pp. 1–29, 2006.

[16] D.-H. Byun, "The AHP approach for selecting an automobile purchase model," *Inf. Manag.*, vol. 38, no. 5, pp. 289–297, 2001.

[17] E. W. T. Ngai, "Selection of websites for online advertising using the AHP," *Inf. Manag.*, vol. 40, no. 4, pp. 233–242, 2003.

[18] U. Cebeci, "Fuzzy AHP-based decision support system for selecting ERP systems in textile industry by using balanced scorecard," *Expert Syst. Appl.*, vol. 36, no. 5, pp. 8900–8909, 2009.

[19] U. S. Bititci, P. Suwignjo, and A. S. Carrie, "Strategy management through quantitative modelling of performance measurement systems," *Int. J. Prod. Econ.*, vol. 69, no. 1, pp. 15–22, 2001.